About the Author

Owen Fitzpatrick is a qualified psychologist, psychotherapist and hypnotherapist. He is the presenter expert on prime time television show *Not Enough Hours* on RTÉ, where each week he works with someone to help them manage their time and lives more effectively. Owen achieved the accolade of becoming the youngest-ever Licensed Master Trainer of Neuro-Linguistic Programming in the world when he was aged just 23. He has trained people on four continents, teaching them how to enhance their lives. Since then, he has evolved into one of Europe's top motivational speakers and personal development trainers and is co-author of *Conversations with Dr Richard Bandler*. He lives in Dublin.

Acknowledgements

My Mam, Marjorie Fitzpatrick, and Gillian McNamara Fowley for your help with looking over the book at short notice.

The fantastic volunteers from last year's *Not Enough Hours* show: Conor, Kate, Siobhan, Gerry, Marina, Michael, Olivia, Margaret, Brian, Ann, Dara, Ray and all your wonderful children.

Teresa, the series producer, for your quite brilliant skills; you are one of the smartest and most professional people I have ever had the pleasure to work with and learn from. The rest of the fantastic team behind *Not Enough Hours*: Sally, Shirley, June, Fiona and Karen, and also to Erin, Aifric, Stephen and Julian. Thanks for all I have learned from you. I eventually got a suitcase!

Cormac and Kieran, two brilliant cameramen who became friends, for all your advice and help. All the crew including John, Paul, Liam, Ray, Peter, Brian, Kevin, Dave. Stephen, Alan, Emmet, Laurence, Anita and Ronan, and all the rest, for making the experience even more special.

RTÉ and especially Grainne McAleer for all your encouragement, support and advice.

Brian Langan and all from Poolbeg for all your help and believing in the book. Mick Minogue for the great cartoons.

Dr Richard Bandler for your genius, your generosity and all you have taught me. John LaValle for all your support, help and all I have learned from you. Dr Glenda Bandler and Kathleen LaValle for being wonderful friends. Brian Colbert and your family Theresa, Dylan, Cian and Karen. My buddy and my second family for everything.

All my extended family and cousins and my sister Emer, Robert, Granny and Uncle Seamus O'Neill for your support and love. O'Neill, number one in Dundrum in 2009.

To AC for being a great reason to switch off. To all my friends around the world for all your support and help with the book, in particular Ed, Dave, Shane, Joe, Sabrina, Cindy, Loz, Kev, Michael, Karl, Aoife, Rab, Kate, Hugh and Michelle.

To all the people who came up to me with kind words about the show for reminding me that it is making a difference.

To my Mam and Dad,
the most important people in my life.
I love you both more than I can ever
express with words.
Thank you for making me realise how
every second counts.

Contents

Foreword

by Dr Richard Bandler

To introduce this book, I feel I must first introduce the man who wrote it. I first met Owen Fitzpatrick when he came to study with me as a teenager. He is one of the students of whom I am very proud. He has always worked very hard and very smart and over the years I have watched him become a great trainer and teacher.

He has helped me to write books, and written two with me as a co-author. I can tell you from personal experience that he knows a lot about organising and utilising time. I have sent clients to him over the years and he has never disappointed me. Owen is a talented agent of change. Having looked over this work, I can see just how Owen has applied all he learned and gone so much further.

I am going to be recommending this book for many years, to my students and to my clients. This work is the quintessential guide to time management. I can say from forty years of labouring to help people find joyful lives, nothing is more important than how you spend the moments of your life.

Most of my clients over the years have wasted far too much time. This book offers you practical and usable steps to spending your time wisely. It is well thought-out, well organised, and readable. What more can you ask from a book that will save you time?

Owen has given you a guide to have more life and more time to achieve your goals and desires. The techniques in this book are proven by the results you will get. Use this book, do the exercises yourself and, I promise you, life will get easier and you will get a lot more done a lot faster.

I am very proud to say, Owen Fitzpatrick, you have done a great job.

And to you, the reader – read this and get on with it.

Dr. Richard Bandler
January 2009

How to Use this Book

Right . . . the irony of asking for your time to spend reading about how you can save time doesn't escape me. So, here's what I'm going to do. I am going to explain here and now what this book is all about and how to get the best out of it, depending on what you are looking for.

I have deliberately made this book as simple, quick-to-read and easy to use as possible. It is packed full of ideas and you can read it from cover to cover in a matter of hours. For best results, follow the exercises and techniques explained within. Let me start by explaining the structure of the book so that you can skip straight to the sections that are of most interest to you immediately.

The **Introduction** is a good place to start. It will introduce you to the basic ideas contained and the importance of taking responsibility for yourself and your experience with time.

This book is divided into different sections. The **first section** sets the scene of our present problems with time. It explores how time-keeping has evolved and looks at how to read your own body clock and how the way you both speak and think of time can help you manage things more effectively.

The **second section** explores how to survive the time crunch. It allows you to discover what time type you are. You will learn which tendencies best suit you and you will understand why you are that way and, most importantly, what to do about it.

Section Three to **Section Six** describe my own four-step time management approach, called the "TimeWise" System: Analyse, Prioritise, Organise and Actualise.

Section Three offers you a simple and effective way of analysing your time. By understanding where your problems with time lie, you can gain a clear perspective on where you need to go. You can find out where you are spending your time and identify what needs to change.

In **Section Four,** you will gain an in-depth understanding of the importance of the key to time management: prioritisation. By looking at the different aspects of prioritising, you will be given a system that works for you and lets you make decisions which will have profound implications for the rest of your life. You'll also learn why, when and how to say "No".

Section Five is where you will be taught how to organise your schedule, plan your weeks and decide how you will deal with incoming tasks.

You will learn, in **Section Six**, how you can begin to actualise what you have learned in the book and immediately implement it in your life. As well as learning how to create your own Plan of Action, I will talk about motivation and building new habits which work for you.

In the final part, **Section Seven,** you will get plenty of tips and time-saving strategies that will be useful for you in the different areas of your life.

Throughout many chapters, you will find **exercises** designed to ensure that you are taking responsibility for how you handle the tasks with which you are faced. If you do the exercises you will get great results and that will help you enormously. If you don't, you won't. It's that simple.

Use this book as a guide to take control over how you spend the time available to you so that you can start allocating more time to things that matter and make every single moment count.

Reading the essential chapters of the system (Sections Three to Six) will take you a couple of hours and doing the exercises might take you a couple more. That's such a short amount of time in comparison to the amount of time saved.

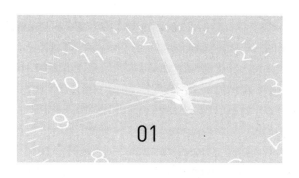

01

Introduction
Welcome to the Time Crisis

*"Time is the cradle of hope . . . Wisdom walks before it,
opportunity with it, and repentance behind it; he that
hath made it his friend will have little to fear from his
enemies, but he who has made it an enemy will have
little to hope from his friends."*

CHARLES CALEB COLTON

YOU ARE NOT SANTA CLAUS. Let me repeat that. YOU
ARE NOT SANTA CLAUS. Now, what do I mean by that?

Okay, every year Santa visits over six billion people
and brings them all presents within 24 hours. That's 250
million people per hour, over four million per minute. He
manages to travel more than a million miles in the same
time period. He has his time management skills honed
and mastered. Plus, he has magical reindeer and magical
powers. And he has 364 days where he doesn't have to travel
or do much work. Who knows? If you had that much time

1

off, maybe you could accomplish what he manages. But you don't . . . and you can't . . . You are NOT Santa Claus.

I feel the need to say that, because some of the people I have met (and even myself from time to time, I must confess) seem to think that we have this same ability to juggle a million things and get them all done. We seem to think every day is just like Christmas Eve and that our cars are our reindeer. We live in a world where we can take on everything all at once and somehow it will get done. When it doesn't happen, we just blame time.

We hear it everywhere: *"There are just not enough hours in the day"* . . . *"I don't have the time"* . . . *"I won't be able to make time for it"* . . . *"I've run out of time"*.

We seem to be living in a temporal famine, with such a scarcity of minutes available that we are running ourselves ragged. Every day we are missing out on more and more of what's important.

We have so much to do, spending what feels like years in traffic, working out our finances, keeping our houses clean, paying our bills, doing the groceries, making our gardens look pretty, booking holidays, emailing, dating, socialising, shopping, playing sports, watching sports, music, the internet . . . Our schedules are packed.

There's work: reports to fill in, forms to sign, meetings to attend, emails to read and send, projects to make progress on, accounts to have in order, targets to hit, presentations to prepare, clients to ring, customers to talk to, paperwork to finish.

Then there's children. Babies who need our full attention every second. School books and uniforms to buy, endless school runs, grinds, breakfasts, lunches, dinners, homework, school activities and societies . . . so many options, so much more to do, so many extra demands on our time. We have so much to manage. It's a wonder we get anything else done. It's exhausting just thinking about it.

A thousand years ago, we had a life expectancy of 45 years of age. Now, we can expect to live to over 80. That's 35 extra years!! That's almost 307,000 extra hours. A thousand years ago, it took many months to travel long distances. Now, we can do it in less than a day.

A thousand years ago, we had little to do but it took a long time to do it. Now, we have lots to do and we can do it far more quickly than before. We should be far more in control of our hours than we were a thousand years ago. However, the opposite is probably more true.

I want to propose in this book that being in control of the hours you spend in the world is not just a matter of applying some techniques but about understanding more about time and learning to adjust how we think about it. To do this, I want to answer certain questions: How did we come to measure time as we do? Where did our years, months and weeks come from? How do our body clocks and things like jetlag work? Why does time seem to go fast and slow in different situations? What is the time crisis? How do we master the use of our time?

The Clock is Ticking

In *Gulliver's Travels*, the little people from Lilliput thought that Gulliver's watch was his god, as he consulted it so much. In many ways, we are just like Gulliver. We go from place to place, continuously referring to the time.

"Time" is the most commonly used noun in the English language. "Year" and "day" are the third and fifth most common nouns respectively.

Have you ever had one of those days? You know the one I'm talking about. Your alarm clock screams at you, "WAKE UP! IT'S TIME TO WAKE UP, OR YOU'LL BE LATE!!" You open your eyes, dazed and confused. You struggle to leave your bed and once you eventually make it up, you are under the eye of the clock.

You go to check your email and do it as quickly as possible; however, it takes you a lot longer than you expected and you rush around knowing you have far less time than you thought.

You grab your keys and then suddenly realise you can't find your phone. You frantically search everywhere and start panicking, fully aware that you are really in trouble. Finally, you call your partner on the phone to see if they took it by mistake when you suddenly realise you are calling them on it. Embarrassed and mildly amused, you sprint out the door, only to freeze again, realising in the commotion that now you are not sure where you left your keys. Minutes later you find them again and you rush, stressed and anxious, into the car.

You find yourself stuck in traffic, fretting about it and stressed out, until you finally arrive in a dazed and nervous heap, unsure of yourself, apologising for your lateness and caught up with excuses.

Most of us can relate to this kind of day. The world is a treadmill and we seem to have lost the controls.

The Need for Speed

Carl Honoré, in his popular book *In Praise of Slow*, argues that we need to slow down. He explains that the world is flying by far too quickly and it is bad for us. By revealing many of the fast-paced lifestyle problems out there, he proposes the idea that we should start appreciating the benefits of slowing down a bit and enjoying the present moment more.

We are so caught up in trying to make everything faster that we find ourselves sacrificing things that are essential for us like regular exercise and a healthy diet. When we do exercise, we try to cram it in and take shortcuts which lead to injuries. We tend to grab food on the run and the lack of nutrients of this "convenience food", plus the way we gobble it down, can have negative effects on our digestive systems.

Furthermore, we find ourselves stuck in a rut where nothing is ever fast enough and anything that slows us down is a disastrous enemy in need of destroying. We get angry if we have to wait even a few extra seconds. Honoré suggests that we live in an "age of rage".

While modern technology helps us free up our time, it has also allowed us to take on so much more. While years ago it took 30 minutes to cook, since the invention of microwaves we can get impatient waiting for our food to cook in 30 seconds.

Nowadays, we can get exceptionally irritated if we have to wait for something. We fail to resist the urge to repeatedly push the button at a zebra crossing or a lift when the button has already been pressed. If we wait more than fifteen seconds, it feels like someone is sadistically torturing us.

Our newfound ability to keep in contact with anyone almost anywhere on the planet means our social networks are changing and we can meet and greet more people more of the time . . . which takes up much more of our time. We have more connections and there is less depth to them.

Many people hold with the ridiculous notion that the busier you are, the more important you are. People wear their "busyness" as something to be eternally proud of. As humans, we are supposed to be active, right? We are supposed to be productive. The idea of having too much to do has developed into a mark of prestige. We aspire to being in the fast lane.

To me, there is nothing wrong with feeling good about being busy, as long as you are busy doing things worth doing. There is something stupid, I think, in being proud of having too much to do and not being able to get it done.

It is important for us to be able to slow down from time to time. In fact, this book is about being able to slow down and even stop for a few moments and examine how your life is going and how you want it to get better.

A study conducted by Richard Wiseman on the pace of life in cities across the globe found that Dublin was the fifth-fastest city in the world for its pace of life. Singapore was number one. A previous study conducted by Robert Levine found that Ireland was the third-fastest country in the world, only beaten by Switzerland and Germany respectively.

We have developed an addiction to doing stuff. Boredom has only been a reality for people for the last two hundred years. Before that, the concept barely existed. With so many choices and things we can do, we feel bad if we don't get one of the things on our menu of options done. We want to do everything, go everywhere, achieve all results, meet everyone; and when we miss out we feel cheated. Time is the enemy that has cheated us.

This need for speed ensures that we have less and less time to take stock of everything. It is easy to end up chasing our tails to keep up. With the ever-expanding options available to us, we are living in a society which suffers from the paradox of choice. There are so many things available to us that we find ourselves feeling worse about all that we don't have instead of being grateful for all that we do have.

The status syndrome, as it has been called, finds us wanting to out-do the neighbours. We want to have a more expensive car, a nicer garden, a larger house. We have a need for status and for looking successful in front of others, in front of our peers.

In order to fund such a lifestyle, we work more and we do more. With the economy turning around, we are left in a more precarious position. We have achieved the status, but we are losing the means to afford the status. So, along comes a financial crisis. The crisis is manageable, but in order to survive we need to learn how best to use our time, which is itself also becoming scarce.

We are left with a richer world, but with far too much going on; we are drowning in a sea of tasks. We are starving for enough hours to do what we want. We are struggling to cope with our very own time crisis.

The Time Crunch

Today, the average person takes on more information in one day than many people did in their entire lifetime in the nineteenth century. The more we can do, the more we take on. It's a cycle which leads us to live in a far faster world than ever before.

We have the same amount of time as we have always had; our problem is that we have the ability to take on far more. So, we do . . . and we stress ourselves, miss quality time, sacrifice time for ourselves and end up burning ourselves out. Then we feel there is nothing we can do, so we resign ourselves to this cruel fate, where there are just not enough hours.

Our time crisis has been with us since long before we noticed any problems with our financial future. They have similar origins. We have invested time into areas of our lives when we don't have enough of it and we find ourselves chasing our tails to keep up, struggling with a time deficit.

I also refer to this time crunch as a crisis because our health is suffering, our families are suffering, our lives are suffering. To counter this, we engage in time binges. Time binges are our efforts to maintain relationships or our health by spending a couple of days every once in a while taking care of things. We try and make up for our lives by these spurts of quality time, but they are not examples of quality time – they are quality examples of fire-fighting. We are not fooling anyone, least of all ourselves.

We are stuck in a rut, unable to know where to go or what to do in order to get out of it. We are so caught up in our busyness that we don't even know how to change.

Some of us are addicted to the office. Some of us take on far too many responsibilities outside of work. Some of us have our time eaten up by commuting and the demands of looking after children. Some of us are trying to juggle different aspects of our lives. But things seem so hard to manage.

In 1969, a Japanese man, Mr Miyazaki, became the first medically documented case of *Karoshi* – which translates as "death from overwork" – who died from working over 4,320 hours per year. It seems the addiction to work can be as dangerous as other addictions. A recent study suggested that Japanese men who work 60 hours a week are twice as likely to have a heart attack than men who work 40 hours a week. It costs hundreds of billions each year in the world economy as more and more people miss work as a result of stress and burnout. Doing too much is bad for us.

It is quite ironic that doctors, who are meeting people suffering from stress everyday, are themselves taking on too much and are suffering stress-related problems as a result.

So, we need help. We need to learn how to manage our lives so that we can juggle things successfully. We need to discover the secrets of using our time in the best possible way. The clock is ticking and it is our time for a change. It is time for us to change our lifestyle.

Handling the New Time Crisis

So, how do we handle this brave new world? How do we handle the need for speed, the preoccupation with status, success, money and drive which seems to permeate our present society? How do we manage to survive and thrive in a world full of overwhelming demands, bombarding us at every junction? Well, the answer comes down to understanding how we can manage our lives better. We need to turn the focus away from **managing "time"** to **managing our lives**.

Although people use the term "time management" extensively to describe ways you can take control of your life, we can't actually "manage" time. We can't order it or tell it what to do or motivate it. All we can do is work within its constraints. We can spend it but we cannot really save it and we certainly cannot control it.

Wouldn't it be fantastic if we could turn back the clock whenever we needed to and do something all over again, even better? To be able to say, "Oi, Time – yeah I'm talking to you! Go back there again, please. I want another chance at that . . ." or "Hey, Time! I'm talking to Mr Ridiculously Boring – could you speed up a bit, please, as this is absolutely agonising?"

Sadly, this is out of our realm of control. So, we are forced to accept the 24 hours as we get them. That is all we get and all we will ever get.

Since we can't organise time, we need to realise that we can only organise ourselves in relation to time. We can't fire time and we can't hire time. All we can do is co-ordinate ourselves and our lives as best we can while dealing with time.

We must learn to manage our life instead of managing our time. Since we can't change time, we must work with it and under its conditions. But the wonderful result in doing this is that when we learn to master working with it, we can maximise our success, wellbeing, productivity and satisfaction with ourselves.

Time management can often seem like a monotonous, laborious and painstaking set of techniques, popular mainly in business. However, it is an integral part of personal coaching and a true cornerstone of life improvement. Mastering how you use your time is really mastering how you live your life.

Many time management books argue that they have a fresh new approach and radical new way of perceiving time. What I've always found is that almost every "new" approach out there is a rehashed version of the basic approach.

Some say that "To Do lists" are a waste of time. Then they call their own "To Do lists" by another name. Some say prioritising is a waste of time and then go on to explain how it's essential that you decide what is most important to you. Some argue that you should slow down and stop living the fast life but dismiss the idea that learning to become more efficient in today's world is a good thing.

This book is different. It is not based upon a radical new technique which works in all cases. Rather, it is based upon all of the tried and tested techniques that work, that get results. It is based upon developing a different attitude towards time and time management. The ideas are drawn from my experience with thousands of people all over the world, helping them manage their time and create happier lives.

I don't claim to be perfect and if you have any need for clarity on that, I can give you plenty of references for my personality flaws. What I do claim to know about is how to help people examine their lives and how to encourage them, will them, influence them, assist them, work with them and, if necessary, provoke them to improve things.

As a psychologist, I have always been fascinated with people and focused on teaching one fundamental truth.

KEY POINT

The way you deal with the world in your mind is the key to a happy and successful life.

If you can get your head together and have the right attitude, you can deal with anything and come through any test. And life *will* test you.

I believe fundamentally that now, more than ever, we really need to master these skills. In a world where our financial security is at risk and the credit crunch threatens to destroy our wealth, it has never been as important for us to learn to focus on maximising how we use our time. We need to be at our best in all areas and we need to make the most of whatever we have got. Unfortunately, sometimes people spend time feeling bad about what they believe they can't control. This book is focused on helping you take back control and responsibility for your own life.

The Two Attitudes Towards Time

The way in which we handle time is largely determined by our **attitude** towards it. Our attitude is the way we think about things. Research has shown that your way of looking at the world plays a key role in how successful you are. People have two key attitudes towards time. Most of us generally switch between one or the other depending on our mood, but we broadly fit into one of these two general mentalities.

We have the choice to live in a blame mentality or a responsibility mentality. When we choose blame we are the victims of our circumstances. When we choose responsibility we decide to control our own destinies.

Some people have a **blame mentality**. They constantly complain about everything regardless of how great things are or aren't. They are the critics to whom nothing is ever good enough. They are never satisfied and they look for what is wrong, broken or flawed. In great economic times, in horrible ones, they always find something to gripe about. These are the people who lament the fact that there are just not enough hours available to them. They are restricted to suffering the sad reality that life is full of too much to do and too little time to do it.

They are the types who would attack the idea of time management because they would prefer to feel bad about how hard things are than to take action to sort it out. In many ways, they are happier when things aren't so good in the economy and in the world because they have more to complain about. And that's what they do. Complain.

13

Of course, these people often aren't aware of this attitude. When challenged, they will usually blame outside circumstances and will claim that they shouldn't have to do anything about it. They will therefore continue to live in a world where they are victims of their circumstances.

Others have a **responsibility mentality**. They are the ones who believe that they are captains of their own ship, controllers of their own destiny. They do not look to the lack of hours they have; rather, they look to all that they can do in the hours they have.

They see time like a field and it is their job to make the most of that field. Essentially, they realise that the time we have is all the time we have got. We have 24 hours a day. We have to make the most of that time. We can improve. We can learn things which make our lives easier. We can build new habits and reap the rewards of such habits.

So, we have the choice: to live in a "blame" mentality, or to live in a "responsibility" mentality. We get to determine how we approach time. But why should we be looking to take responsibility? Why not just accept the harshness that life imposes on us and accept our lives for how they are? Why bother improving?

The answer is simple. Because we can. If we can make things easier and more fun and make ourselves happier, then the real question is, why not?

The Simplicity of Change

In the self-improvement field, there are many different ideas out there that emphasise a switch in thinking. Books such as *The Secret* and *The Power of Now* offer very simple ideas that can help you change your life. *The Secret* suggests that you can attract what you want in life by focusing on it, while *The Power of Now* offers you a happier life if you "live in the present moment". It is in these simple attitude switches that our lives can be turned around and we can find happiness, inner peace and success.

We yearn for a simple and direct way to change everything and these simple ideas appeal to us. Of course, the cynics argue vehemently against the draw of such simple concepts, arguing that the world is far more complicated than these theories make out.

However, change is often simple. It involves being aware of what you are doing, learning to do something else instead and disciplining yourself to continue doing the new behaviour until it becomes a habit. Changing the way you handle time is the very same process. To start this process, it is essential that you take responsibility for changing things around yourself.

KEY POINT

Change is simpler than you think. It involves being aware of what you are doing, learning to do something else instead and disciplining yourself to continue doing the new behaviour until it becomes a habit.

Not Enough Hours

Not Enough Hours is the lifestyle television series on RTÉ. One in which I work with someone each week and help them to manage their time better. The series was designed for modern-day commuters, families and businesspeople who struggle with all that they have to get done each day.

What began in the offices of RTÉ continued all around the country, from Kildare to Galway, Kilkenny to Longford. In the first series, I met eight different families and worked with a terrific television crew. I spent many hours preparing, watching DVDs of footage of the clients in the show and figuring out with the producer how best to present the problem and solution for camera.

I met a workaholic who spent up to 20 hours working per day; a hair salon owner who couldn't say "No"; a college student who was always late; and a mother who took on every task herself and wouldn't allow her husband to help. I was introduced to a sports journalist who filled up his days with worries about the future; a perfectionist who often hoovered at midnight and was obsessed with eating healthily while missing out on other important things; an artist with dyspraxia who felt permanently "lost" in time; and a working couple who found themselves stuck in a rut in a never-ending routine.

During this book, you will meet these characters. You will also learn how they changed and discover how to apply the techniques that worked for them in your own life.

During the show, there are some nuggets of advice available for the viewer at home, as well as, hopefully, a bit of entertainment. The people in the programme looking for help are the stars of each show and the viewers are asked to identify with their journey.

I teach people how to manage their time and life so they have more time for the things that really matter. I don't believe in telling people what they "should" do. I prefer the concept of helping them realise what they "can" do.

Some suggest that we should just accept our lot and learn to be okay with what we have and who we are. Of course, I agree that we should learn to be happy with who we are and accept ourselves, but we should also remember that we can improve in any area once we learn what the disciplines are, and practise them.

Every successful person in the history of the world has decided to improve their lot, in spite of the circumstances. If you don't want to, then that's your choice. If you do want to, then there are ideas out there which can help you do just that.

When I work with someone, I have two important goals in mind for effective time management: **time wealth** and **time value**. Time wealth is how much time you have available to you. I want to show you, as you take the journey of reading this book, that you have much more time available to you once you sort out what's most important. Time value is what quality time you have available to you. I also want to explain how you can make the most of every moment you have by learning to use your mind in a new way.

Each time I refer to **quality time** in this book, let me be very clear about what I mean, since the term is thrown about a lot.

Quality time is time you spend with yourself or with others which you feel means something and adds value to your life.

In other words, quality time is time that you spend with someone that makes you feel closer to them and where you get to enjoy yourself with them. This could include spending time with yourself! This means time where you felt it meant something and possibly an experience you will fondly remember in the future.

What I want to do in this book is the same thing that I do on the show. I want to offer you suggestions that will make your life simpler, more organised and happier if you follow them. Of course, they will only work if you follow them.

The Promise of Being TimeWise

The secret of getting the best out of your time is pretty simple, actually. When you take a little time to apply a few basic techniques, you can be far smarter and wiser in how you manage your life. I want to introduce you to my system, the **TimeWise** system. This approach, as I have mentioned previously, is based upon the system I used with the people I worked with on the show and is made up of the key concepts of time management. It works like this.

You figure out where and how you spend your time. You **analyse** what you are doing, what you have to do and what you want to do. Next, you figure out what is most important to you. You **prioritise** your activities. You get yourself **organised** with schedules and learn to plan effectively. Lastly, you implement the changes to your lifestyle and you create an **action plan** for yourself that allows you to run your life in the way that you desire.

That is really the step-by-step process, but I want to guide you through this process in such a way that you will discover a new way of thinking about time.

The truth is that using time in the best possible way is not difficult. I'm a simple thinker. A lot of the principles and ideas contained here are based on common sense. But the thing about common sense is that it isn't always very common. Taking a little time reading this book will save you a massive amount of time in the rest of your life.

It is in our mentality to feel the scarcity of available time. Our minds crave more and more things to do. So time becomes our enemy, as it restricts us from doing these things. It is not a question of there being enough hours but of how we spend those hours. Our problem is not a shortage of time but how we use the time we have and how we feel about the time we use. Of course, our ambitions and lofty ideals are a good thing. The trick is to learn to feel good about time by accepting the limitations of time, as a positive aid to our focus and concentration. We must learn to enjoy the time we spend and to spend it in a way that helps us to grow and allows us to take control of our lives.

Being wise about time means learning to identify what you need to improve and how you can improve. It is about achieving the perfect balance between what you need to do and what you want to do so you have time for the things that truly matter. It is about making the most of your life. But I must warn you, there are side-effects of using this system. You could find yourself enjoying life more and you might just become ridiculously happy.

Firstly, though, let's explore some more about the fascinating subject of time. We live in a very different world than we did thousands of years ago. What exactly is our relationship with time now? Well, it seems that we are struggling. It seems as if we are running out of time.

SECTION 1

RUNNING OUT OF TIME

02

The Need for Time

"I hate clocks . . . A clock to my life is like a hen to a
naked man, sunburnt and covered in corn."

Somewhere off the western coast of England,
28 miles from Land's End,
7.10 p.m., Wednesday 22nd October, 1707

It was a dark, rainy evening when a sailor aboard the
HMS Association urgently visited the ship's captain and
the commander-in-chief of the British Naval Fleets, Sir
Cloudesley Shovell.

Sir Cloudesley was leading a fleet of ships back to
Britain after a battle against the French, an unsuccessful
attempt to capture the town of Toulon. The sailor, a
native of the Scilly Isles, anxiously reported that he could
smell a familiar smell from his homelands. He could sense
that they were dangerously close to the islands.

The captain dismissed the sailor's concerns, as the clock he referred to suggested that they were nowhere near the longitude that the sailor reported. They used a principle known as dead reckoning, which worked by using the trajectory of the ship and the accuracy of the clock to predict where they were. By this principle, they were safely out at sea. They couldn't be that close to the islands. It was impossible.

Unfortunately, it was not. That night at around about 8.00 p.m., four ships of the fleet, including the *HMS Association*, brutally crashed into the rocks and more than a thousand people died at sea. Legend has it that Sir Cloudesley himself survived, only to be killed on one of the islands' shores by someone who robbed him for his priceless emerald ring.

More than a thousand people dead, one of the worst British maritime disasters of all time, and all because of an inaccurate method of keeping time. Seven years later, the British government offered a large reward for anyone who could invent a clock that provided a more effective and reliable measurement of time, and thus of longitude. Later that century, John Harrison, a carpenter turned clockmaker, began to work on such a project and created a brilliantly workable clock which proved much more reliable than ever before.

Thus, our accurate measurement of time became more and more important. Over the next few centuries, this continued as our systems of transport changed and the Industrial Revolution formalised a more structured way to work. Nowadays, we carry watches, phones and iPods everywhere we go and we use them as a reminder to ourselves of what time it is.

In order to work with time in a more effective way, it is a good idea to learn more about it. When we wake up in the morning, the first thing we do is to check the time. The question "What time is it?" has been asked by billions of people worldwide. For some, it is a genuine attempt to learn what time it is. For others, it is simply a means to an end – to successfully engage someone in a conversation.

The origins of our present way of telling what time it is comes from a system which has been honed and mastered over centuries. There has been a quest for more accurate clocks in an attempt by us to try and add more structure to the nature of the universe.

Back to the Future

It's fascinating to examine the true **nature of time** and the different ideas that scientists have to explain it. I have always been fascinated by time travel. I watched movies like *Back to the Future* again and again as a child and also loved the recent thriller *Déjà Vu*. The idea that somehow we could change the past – that we had the opportunity to go back in time and make things work out differently – was very appealing to me.

In "reality", we think of time as going forward and time travel is generally viewed as impossible. At the same time, there are many theorists out there who optimistically suggest that, as modern technology advances, we will find a way to do so. Regardless, in the west, we perceive time as going in one direction.

Since Einstein, scientists have argued that space and time are relative and that, because of this, the future, past and present all exist already. Since we are moving from the past into the future, this presupposes that the future exists for us to move into it. Quantum physicists have since dismissed this possibility, suggesting instead that future time grows out of the past and that time does not flow as previously assumed.

Time occurs at a different speed depending on how far away from the Earth that you are. Gravity tends to have a subtle effect on how much time goes by. If you were to travel into space and arrive back, you would have experienced less time elapsing than someone on the ground.

Although I have a grasp of the basics, whenever I read more in depth into the physics of time, I'd be lying if I said I understand the physicists who discuss the true nature of time. It goes way over my head. Suffice it to say that our understanding of how time works is still far from complete but, despite that fact, we still handle it reasonably well. We don't need to understand it perfectly.

There are all sorts of theories that discuss parallel universes, black holes, worm holes and the real possibility of time travel. If you want to read more deeply on the matter, you can do so. What I want to do, to put things in context, is examine how our way of thinking about time came about. I also want to argue how we can affect our own futures.

Bear with me on this: if the future is the future of the present then the present is the past of the future. So, we

26

change the future by doing what we do in the present. The only difference is, since we don't know what's in store in the future, we aren't changing it; we are creating it. We have an impact on our futures. Some theorists go so far as to propose that time only exists in our minds. All we have is the present; the future and past exist solely in our own heads.

To me, the beauty of the programme *Not Enough Hours* is that it gives me an opportunity to get inside the heads of the people I work with and to paint pictures of potential futures that lie in store. Part of my role is akin to that of the Ghost of Christmas Future, with the obvious difference that I dress slightly better than that character did in the Dickens's *A Christmas Carol*. (I figured that if I wore a black robe and brought them to the cemetery, it might have a completely different effect than the one I was looking for.)

Getting people to see into their futures is not a magic trick; it is something we do all the time. The key is that when you see your future as it will be if you keep on the same road you are on, it is a powerful enough experience to get you to stop and think about things.

The Beginning of Time

The past, the present and the future are all fascinating aspects of time and the notion that the past and future exist only inside our heads is an interesting one. But what about our **measurement of time**? How have we organised time? Well, the organisation of time goes back thousands of years, to when we first learned to tell what time, day and season it was.

Ancient cultures measured time by the position of the sun, the moon and the stars.

In July 2006, I had the wonderful experience of visiting Cairo. I remember walking around the pyramids, fascinated to see these wonderful, inspiring structures created so precisely and so terrifically. The question was, how? How did the ancient Egyptians manage to create such architecturally brilliant designs with very primitive means?

The ancient Egyptians, as well as the Babylonians, were very advanced in many different areas – for example, measuring time. They needed to find ways of organising and co-ordinating communal activities and events, scheduling the movement of goods, and planting and harvesting.

As I wandered around the many historical sites in Egypt, I learned more and more about the ancient system of organising calendars that they used back then. From early evidence of sundials and recording of lunar waterclocks, we can see that up to 5,000 years ago the Egyptians had their own way of understanding time.

Many of the ancient cultures had fascinating ways of looking at time. There are a number of different calendars in the world that reveal different dates for today – Islamic, Jewish and Mayan Calendars, to name but a few. The earliest calendars were based loosely around the various season cycles. Indeed, our own calendar comes from a mixture of influences including the ancient Egyptian calendar as well as Jewish and Roman influences. The BC (Before Christ) and AD (Anno Domini) distinctions obviously come from the Christian Church.

What Date Is It?

We seem to take the date for granted, but interestingly enough, we have only started measuring dates as we do in the last few hundred years. We follow a calendar known as the Gregorian Calendar after Pope Gregory XIII. He established this calendar, which took effect in most Catholic states in 1582. However, it was only adopted by Britain, Ireland and the United States in 1752.

Let's have a look at the difference between the various calendars out there. For example, the date Friday, 1 May 2009 in our calendar corresponds to the following dates:

- Julian Calendar: 18 April 2009

- Chinese: Cycle 78, year 26 (Ji-Chou), month 4 (Ji Si), day 7 (Bing-Wu)

- Hebrew: 7 Iyar 5769

- Discordian: Sweetmorn, Discord 48, Year of Our Lady of Discord 3175

- Islamic Calendar: 6 Jumada I-Ula, 1430

- Mayan Calendar: 12.19.16.5.10

> It's fascinating to think that when we talk about various dates, there are many different ways of describing them. We are reminded every year that we only have one of many different calendars when we hear that the Chinese New Year falls in late January or early February.
>
> Another interesting feature of the Chinese calendar is that the date of your birth determines what kind of personality you are supposed to have. Your astrological sign has become a popular personality guide. Also, the year of your birth is an important year by which to be categorised. I was born in the Year of the Horse. According to Chinese astrology, I am funny, strong, handsome, clever, fun to be with, full of energy and a natural athlete. So, obviously, I think that the Chinese year of birth is a very accurate way of evaluating personality.

In our present calendar, one year equals approximately 365 days, with one extra day every four years. Within each of these days are 24 hours, giving a total of 8,760 hours per year. Multiplying this by 60 minutes per hour, we get 525,600 minutes per year. Breaking it down even further, we get 31,536,000 seconds in a year's timespan.

That is a massive amount of time that we have at our disposal. Often, however, it doesn't seem like we do. Our time seems taken up on other tasks and problems. So, why is the year broken up into months and weeks and days? Where does all that come from? Let's look at the structure of our year.

What's Another Year?

I was too young to remember seeing Johnny Logan winning his first Eurovision Song Contest with his exceptionally depressing song "What's Another Year?". I'm glad of that actually. The lyrics refer to how he's lost everything and is crying all the time and is used to being alone, so what does one more year matter?

Well, I think that if Johnny took control over his life, then he could turn things around in a year. In fact, I'm sure winning the Eurovision helped. A lot can happen in a year. But where exactly did years come from?

Thousands of years ago, our ancestors needed to have some system that let them know when the seasons would come about for agricultural reasons. They needed to know when the different types of weather were expected for planting, harvesting and hunting. Thus, they created a calendar based upon two main systems: the solar year and the lunar month.

The solar year was the time it took for the Earth to travel around the Sun. In those days, their understanding was purely based upon the Sun's location and they estimated that one year had passed when the Sun was in the same position again. In terms of which season it was, this was measured by a crude combination of the position of the Sun and the temperature or amount of rain at the time.

The solar day was also something that was immediately noticed back then. There was a period of light when it was possible to find food, hunt and eat. This was then followed by a period of darkness, which seemed to go hand-in-hand with sleep.

The solar day and night were divided into 24 hours. This came about as a result of a custom of the Egyptians. They used to mark every ten days with the appearance of constellations of stars called decans. At the annual flooding of the Nile, as a star called Sirius rose, 12 decans could be seen in the sky.

The number 12 was determined to be a special, significant number and the period of dark each night was divided into twelve equal parts. Soon, the day was divided similarly and these hours were known as temporal hours, as their duration depended on the length of days and nights, which changed in different seasons.

The month, a word directly connected to the Moon, is the time it takes for a moon to go through the cycle from being full to diminishing and then returning to a full moon again.

However, where the concept of a week came from is more controversial. Some suggest that the Babylonians divided each month into the four patterns of the movement of the Moon. Others argue that the Old Testament proposed the idea that God created the world in seven days and that this became a desired method of dividing time.

Probably the most convincing theory also explains where the names of each day of the week came from. By the time of the Romans, there were a number of known "planets" in the sky. These planets were known as Mars, Mercury, Venus, Jupiter and Saturn. They also included the Sun and Moon, which were perceived to be planets as well. All in all, there were seven of them. Thus, it was determined that there be seven days.

Now, each day had 24 hours at that stage and each hour was named after one of the planets. The planets were listed in order of the length of time they took to "rotate" around the earth. The hierarchy went as follows: Saturn, Jupiter, Mars, the Sun, Venus, Mercury and then the Moon.

On day one, the first hour was called Saturn, the second hour was Jupiter, the third Mars and so on. This sequence was continued over and ran straight into the next day. So, on day two, the first hour was Sun. Each day had a different planet to start their day.

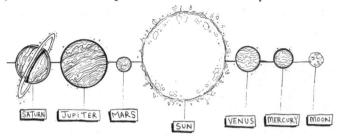

Day One	Day Two	Day Three
Hour 1: Saturn	Hour 1: Sun	Hour 1: Moon
Hour 2: Jupiter	Hour 2: Venus	Hour . . . etc.
Hour 3: Mars	Hour 3: Mercury	
Hour 4: Sun	Hour 4: Moon	
Hour 5: Venus	Hour 5: Saturn	
Hour 6: Mercury	Hour 6: Jupiter	
Hour 7: Moon	Hour 7: Mars	
Hour 8: Saturn	Hour 8: Sun	
Hour 9: Jupiter	Hour 9: Venus	
Hour . . . etc.	Hour . . . etc.	
Hour 23: Jupiter	Hour 23: Venus	
Hour 24: Mars	Hour 24: Mercury	

These "first" planets soon became the dominant planet of the day until each day was named after their dominant planet. So, we had Saturn, Sun, Moon, Mars, Mercury, Jupiter and Venus in that order. Latin-based languages stay close to these words to this day. For example, in French the days of the week are: *samedi*, *dimanche*, *lundi*, *mardi*, *mercredi*, *jeudi* and *vendredi*. In English, however, the names of the last four days of the week were renamed after Anglo-Saxon gods: Tiw, Woden, Thor and Frig.

Finally, the Babylonians used the number 60 in their astronomical calculations. They favoured counting in units of 60, as 60 can be divided into two equal parts of 30, three equal parts of 20, four equal parts of 15, five equal parts of 12 or six equal parts of 10. Its highly divisible nature made it an ideal number to work with.

This was soon adopted by the Romans to divide up hours. Each hour was split into 60 "first small divisions" – "prima minuta" – which became known as minutes and then divided each minute into 60 "second small divisions" or "seconda minuta", which was soon shortened to seconds.

To sum up, we have years, which came about as a result of the Earth's journey around the Sun. We have months, which resulted from the movement of the Earth in relation to the Moon. Weeks were concerned with what was understood to have been the seven planets of the sky. Days were connected with the periods of light and dark (caused by the Earth's rotation). Hours, minutes and seconds were the measurements of the day and night. So, now that we understand how we arrived at our present structure of time measurement, how exactly has time been measured?

The Birth of Clocks

As I saw in the Egyptian tombs, hours were first measured during the daytime by sundials and at night-time by waterclocks. By the movement of the Sun's shadow and the flowing of water, we learned how many hours had passed. I found this fascinating, imagining what it would have been like to live in a world where we could only guess at what time it was.

In medieval times, we began to use more and more sophisticated methods of telling the time. In the thirteenth century, the mechanical clock came into existence with the first clock in 1283 in Bedfordshire, England. Almost 400 years later, it was discovered that pendulums were a potentially useful tool for measuring time. The first pendulum clock was devised by Christian Huygens on Christmas Day in 1656. It was, by far, the most accurate clock created. Whereas previous clocks had an error to correct of about 15 minutes per day, pendulum clocks had an error of one minute per week.

From then on, pendulums were used consistently to make the clock a more accurate device. After the British government offered a reward for a more accurate timepiece, inventor John Harrison made great strides by creating his own clock, which was far more accurate than its predecessors.

More and more exact ways of telling the time became very important to the Industrial Revolution in the nineteenth century, where the working hours of the average person came under scrutiny. Suddenly, we were thrown into a world in which we were accountable for every minute we spent.

Nowadays, clocks have come so close to approximating the exact time that scientists have created an atomic clock. This is so accurate that it is only out by one second every 300 million years.

We have digital watches which display the time in digits and analogue watches which display the time by three hands going around a circular clock. One hand is for hours, one for minutes and one for seconds.

Furthermore, as we carry around a close approximation of time with us on digital and analogue watches, on mobile phones, Blackberries, iPods and laptops, we are constantly aware of what time it is and, when we aren't, we will habitually ask others.

In many ways we are becoming slaves to our watches, victims of our clocks, running vigorously as time runs out on us. We find ourselves chasing our tails to keep up with the ever-pressing demands of a society where speed is the motto and time is money.

Before clocks, we lived on what has been described by sociologists as "**natural time**", where we ate when we were hungry and slept when we were tired. The comedian Tommy Tiernan calls this "Farmer Time" – as he explains it, farmers do the things they need to do rather than trying to live up to a schedule. Now, we face a conflict between what time our bodies tell us it is and when our "real" clocks tell us it is time to do something.

We have schedules and routines and have to do things at certain times and be somewhere at other times. Frederick Taylor's concept of "**scientific management**" – a system of working more efficiently by maximising how long and hard workers worked – was adopted and further pushed us into a time trap. We are expected to do as much as we can possibly do and push ourselves to the maximum every second.

The problem is that our bodies are not meant to function in such a society. By pushing ourselves as hard as we do, more and more people are burning out. We have so much to do and are figuratively and literally killing ourselves to do it all.

Learning from our past can help us improve our future. We need to understand that this "slavery" to the clock did not always exist and that we can learn to think outside of it while working with it.

Daylight Savings Time

September 1999, West Bank, Palestinian Territory

It was a typical busy day in September, 1999. In the West Bank, Daylight Savings Time was due to end on Friday, 15 October. Meanwhile, in Jerusalem, Israel switched back to standard time on Friday, 3 September. Hence, there was an hour's difference between the two areas, which are separated by a wall. This time difference was to kill three people and save many more.

Terrorists from the West Bank prepared time bombs and smuggled them to their counterparts in

Jerusalem, who misunderstood the time on the bombs. As the bombs were being planted, they exploded one hour too early, killing three terrorists instead of the intended victims – two busloads of people.

Daylight Savings Time was invented to allow us to have an extra hour of sunlight in the winter and has proved useful in a number of ways. But not every country uses this system. In fact, many countries have their own cultural ways of working with and thinking about time.

Cultural Time

While certain circumstances and our own body clocks affect how we perceive and experience time, depending on the culture we live in, they also affect how we deal with this fascinating creature. In order to truly manage the time you have in the best possible way, it's useful to explore around the world to observe how people think about time.

Irish Standard Time

We Irish have always been masterful at communicating with double meaning. Joyce, Yeats and Wilde all excelled at this. While British English or American English offer concrete "yes" and "no" answers and a more precise way of speaking, Irish English uses metaphors and vague terms that capture the imagination of the listener without actually ascribing to any dogma.

The Irish sense of time is similarly different. (Sorry, I couldn't resist!) Above Shandon Church in Cork, there are famous clocks called the Four-Faced Liars. These four clocks, one on each side of the tower, show slightly different times to each other.

Irish standard time has long been known as largely differing from Greenwich Mean Time. Up to thirty years ago, a promise to do some work was as fluid as water and expressions like "at some stage", "soon" or "in a while" could mean anything from minutes to months. We have always been traditionally relaxed about time in this country. As a nation whose identity has been repressed for hundreds of years, we still have an underlying resistance to following any rigid system.

Up until 50 years ago, we were still predominantly an agrarian nation, and agriculture was our main focus. For the last 50 years we have been speeding through our own micro industrial revolution into the modern-day technological revolution and we are fast becoming accustomed to this new emphasis on time keeping.

There is a present climate of work obsession. The crucial thing is that we don't find ourselves becoming slaves to the clock and that we remember our priorities. While we can adhere to deadlines, we must not allow them to kill our spirit of freedom, our easy-going nature and our rebellious instincts. That is what makes us Irish.

Western Time

In most countries of the western world, there is a respect for time that has been heralded since the

Industrial Revolution left its mark. The origins of industry and factory work meant that people were to be held more accountable for the exact time they began and finished work.

Nowadays, flight, train and bus schedules are tightly controlled and there is a great emphasis on punctuality. In countries such as Britain and Northern Europe, there is a clear need to define the proper time. Greenwich Mean Time or whatever the country's standard time is the time to which to compare your watch and five minutes slower or faster than that is wrong – not different.

In most of these countries, if you are late you are frowned on and looked down upon. Punctuality is a sign of respect and being late is thus a sign of disrespect. For example, in countries such as Germany or Switzerland, the adherence to exactness is certainly a part of their culture. In business, structure is essential, as is good organisation and people are often fired for poor punctuality.

In America and Europe, most people have a nine-to-five job and do overtime. Working on weekends is becoming more and more popular and days which were once kept sacred are no longer so. We are fast changing to a seven-day working week in our growing marketplace.

In the Mediterranean countries such as Spain and Italy, time is more relaxed but even this depends on what part of that country you are in. For example, in the south of Italy, they have a much more relaxed perception of life and time, whereas in the north, they seem to have a faster "city" mentality. Lateness is more frowned upon in the urban centres of Milan, whereas people from the south are far more accepting and forgiving.

Eastern Time

Since ancient times, the east has had a completely different perspective on time. Time has traditionally been seen as circular in eastern countries. The Hindu and Buddhist philosophies of reincarnation remind us of this preference. The time arrow metaphor – where time is seen as going in one direction, from past to future – which has been favoured in the west has never held much ground in the east until fairly recently. Nowadays, as Japan has already fit into the capitalistic, work-oriented, success-focused culture of the western world, the new emerging countries such as China and India are following suit.

In Japan, the trains are exceptionally organised and punctual, arriving almost exactly to the second. Transport punctuality is very important in Japan. Their culture of professionalism and convenience means that they strive to work perfectly.

However, for thousands of years the Japanese have perceived time as existing in a circular structure where life goes through a cycle of stages, a far cry from the arrow theory of the west. The Japanese have a remarkable ability to tolerate paradox. They are open to two opposing things being true at the same time. This is what we call fuzzy logic. It is the logic that keeps us sane when we try to understand the quantum universe.

So, Japan holds two opposing perspectives of time simultaneously and quite comfortably. China and India are still catching up with the Japanese ability to stick rigidly to deadlines, although most of the reports from the Beijing Olympics praised the efficiency of the people of China.

In places such as India and many South American countries such as Brazil, time is a much more flexible concept. The first time I talked at a workshop in India, in the summer of 2003, I sent them on their first tea break for ten minutes and most of them came back 40 minutes later. It was then that I learned about IST or Indian Standard Time. Indian Standard Time is the "actual" time, plus or minus about 40 minutes or so. It is a flexible measure, like I had been used to in Ireland, but if anything even more flexible.

Timeless Cultures

There is a tribe in the heart of the Brazilian Amazon jungle known as the Pirahã, who don't seem to have any concept of time. Everything for this tribe seems to exist in the present, although in order for any culture to survive it is obviously necessary for them to know that certain actions they take will result in specific outcomes which would allow them to hunt effectively.

Although they struggle with the concept of numbers and counting, the Piraha have various practices they use to ward off evil spirits, which suggests that they have either experienced evil spirits in the past or can conceive of these spirits returning in the future. They do not seem to have the concept of time in their language, however, and speak in an entirely present tense. It's intriguing to think about what our own culture would be like without its regimented structure of daily tasks to do.

As you can see, there are many different cultural perspectives on time. It is also important to note that the context affects the importance of punctuality and time-keeping. We must learn to become aware of the expectations of those around us and work things out effectively for ourselves.

Tips for Embracing Your Time Culture

1 Pay attention to the contexts and the cultures you are involved in and make sure you adhere to their rules of punctuality.

2 Learn how others like to structure their time and work with them. Be flexible.

3 Do your best to fit your own schedule in with your natural time. Sleep when you are tired and eat when you are hungry.

4   Find out ways to influence the immediate culture you live in. See if it is possible to work at home or work different hours.

5   Identify areas in your life where you can begin to slow down, maybe in terms of how you eat, how you exercise or how you spend quality time. It's important to get out of the habit of rushing all the time.

It is also useful to realise that as well as us having to learn to work with the clock of the physical world, we also need to adapt to our individual clock, which lies deep within us.

03

How to Read Your Body Clock

"Sometimes your body is smarter than you are."

ANON

Do you ever wake up ten seconds before your alarm clock goes off? That's because we all have our own internal **biological clock,** which keeps track of time for us in a very accurate way. This clock is, however, very different from another method of time-keeping we possess, which is our ability to estimate time intervals. In order to take control over how we use our time, let us examine more closely these two different systems of time measurement in our bodies.

A couple of years ago, I organised my schedule so that one weekend I was teaching a workshop in Bogota, Colombia. During the following week I had a meeting in Dublin and the following weekend I was teaching in Osaka, Japan. Thus, in the space of seven days, I would be working in three different time zones, 14 hours apart, and travelling over 21,000 miles to do so.

My flight left on Monday afternoon from Bogota and I arrived into Dublin on Tuesday evening. After spending Wednesday in Dublin, I left for Osaka on Thursday morning and arrived on Friday morning, Japanese time. I was absolutely shattered. For the next few days, I was exhausted during the day and wide awake at night time. It was all I could do to stay awake and present as best I could while teaching during the day, even resorting to sleeping during the lunch break.

Furthermore, I was run down and I felt sick and unwell. My body felt as if it had been battered. It got to the point where I felt like I was hallucinating. I was experiencing a particularly strong case of "jet lag".

Jet lag occurs when our biological clock is knocked out of synchronisation. However, jet lag isn't the only such problem that we face in modern society. Our continuous stream of work and multiple hectic schedules have caused us to work all hours and run our bodies through routines it is not used to. From week to week, many of us have a different set of activities to do. Our body clock is being pushed around. This is a kind of "work lag".

Another significant problem we have with time management is our habitually poor ability to estimate how much time passes. Our method of measuring intervals lacks accuracy and can cause us to become disorganised and scatterbrained. Understanding more about your brain and your body's way of measuring time will help you to get a better sense of time, as well as improving your performance by educating you on how and when your body works at its best. Let's examine the two kinds of internal clocks which work in our brains and bodies.

Our Interval Stopwatch: How We Measure Time

The first system for tracking time that we use is an interval stopwatch. This interval stopwatch works inside our minds and allows us to figure out how much time elapses during different events throughout the day. It allows us to track the time it takes for something to happen or to do something.

We all have the ability to measure **interval time**. For example, our concept of rhythm is explained by our ability to judge time. Interval time also allows us to understand what a person means when they say they will call back in five minutes, even without a clock.

The problem is that our in-built ability to measure time deliberately throughout the day is often problematic and varies from person to person and depending on the circumstances and environment. Some people seem to have a much better perception of how much time elapses between two set points while others have little clue.

The interval stopwatch works in an area of the brain known as the basal ganglia. Here, through the combination of millions of connections and a release of the neuro-transmitter dopamine, the brain manages to start and stop periods of time and make an estimate as to the length of time that has passed.

This is not always a perfect system and certain states of mind can create an experience of time distortion, which we will discuss later. Suffice it to say right now that our conscious ability to figure out how much time passes is something that we haven't mastered.

However, we do have an internal clock which works far more accurately than this interval stopwatch. This internal clock works unbeknownst to ourselves. Our bodies keep this clock running and we are only aware of the effects it has on us. It is known as the circadian rhythm.

The Circadian Rhythm: Our 24-Hour Body Clock

The **circadian rhythm** refers to our natural daily biological cycle or body clock. It works closely to a 24-hour cycle and establishes our need for rest and activity. It regulates our patterns of working and resting.

Although the circadian rhythm works independent of external influences, it is continuously reset by daylight, which keeps it in alignment with our natural cycles of day and night. That is why changing time zones has an impact on our body clocks.

This rhythm is affected by the presence of light, which resets the clock. The way daylight affects the clock is an interesting process. The circadian rhythm works in an area of the brain known as the hypothalamus. Here, there are two clusters of brain cells known as the suprachiasmatic nuclei or the SCN. These cells regulate the daily cycle of our bodies and this cycle closely approximates our 24-hour day. There are glial cells in the retina of the eyes and receptors in the skin which pass information to the SCN in terms of the amount of light present.

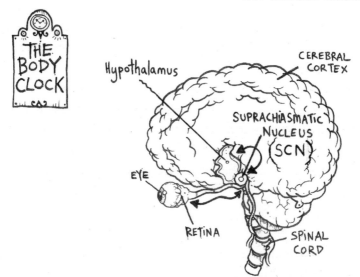

An interesting study from the Cornell Sleep Research Laboratory discovered that simply shining a light at the back of the knees of sleeping subjects also heavily influenced the circadian rhythm, which suggests that it is not simply our eyes that have pathways to the SCN. So light somehow makes its way to the SCN and therefore our body clocks are reset.

The SCN is also the crucial factor involved in the timing regulation of blood pressure and body temperature. Meanwhile, we have other rhythms in all the organs of the body. The heart and liver, for example, run off two different clocks. The liver clock is influenced by changes in eating times, stress, exercise and environmental temperature changes. This explains somewhat the reason why we can get stomach pains when we are not sleeping enough or when we have travelled long distances.

Many of the daily regulatory functions in the body are carried out by the SCN. For example, body temperature rises as the day comes to an end, presumably as an aid to help people fall asleep. It then drops to its lowest before we awake in the morning, again probably related to our need to awaken. The SCN also allows the brain's pineal gland to release a chemical known as melatonin at around 9.00 p.m., which helps us to feel sleepy, and to stop its release at around 7.30 in the morning.

The main circadian rhythm present in the SCN regulates our daily waking cycles by promoting **clock-dependent alerting**. Clock-dependent alerting, coined by a pioneer in the field of sleep research, William Dement, is the main function of our circadian rhythm. It refers to the role this rhythm plays in keeping us awake rather than putting us to sleep and waking us.

The SCN actually works by promoting wakefulness in the body over a cycle of 24 hours. Our bodies are designed naturally to sleep and the circadian rhythm promotes clock dependent alerting, which ensures that we are awake right throughout the day. This has important consequences for those of us interested in understanding more about the best times of the day for us to carry out certain tasks.

The "graveyard shift" describes a period after lunch where people find themselves struggling to stay awake. Previous beliefs suggested that this was a result of the body needing a rest to digest food. Actually, it is more a case of our body clock switching off its clock-dependent alerting as part of the natural cycle.

In 1997, Joseph Takahashi and his colleagues at North-western University discovered the presence of a gene related to our body's clock. This soon became known as the "clock gene". It was soon discovered that the clock gene exists throughout the body in almost every tissue and organ.

This explains how the circadian rhythm determines that different bodily functions are performed at certain times. In fact, we have a number of circadian rhythms, all with their own responsibilities. Although some of the daily rhythms can be changed by us and adjust regardless of the light and dark cycles, there are certain bodily functions which always occur in response to the light or darkness of the day. These include melatonin secretion and cortisol release as well as the regulation of blood pressure and body temperature. It's fascinating how this works. There are even certain times of the day when you are more likely to get different illnesses. Hayfever, for example, is often more prominent in the morning than it is later in the day. Research suggests that babies are more likely to be born at 4.00 a.m. than at any other time of day, whereas people are statistically more likely to die at 5.00 a.m.

Get into a routine to keep your body clock in synch. Avoid changing around too much when you sleep, eat and wake up. Your body needs consistency.

Understanding the circadian rhythm is important as it allows you to understand how your body works best and ensures that you take into account your own natural clock when structuring activities in the real world. One of these important activities is sleep.

Our Need for Sleep

One of the greatest victims of our need to make the most of every minute is sleep. The positive benefits of a good night's sleep include being happier and healthier and being less susceptible to colds, flus and psychological problems. Sleep deprivation can lead to fatal accidents, such as the Exxon Valdez oil spill, where a report found sleep deprivation to be the primary cause of the disaster. Sleep deprivation is also partly and often fully to blame in many road accidents ever year.

The problem is that sleep deprivation is no longer just something that night-shift workers or students face at exam time; it is something that most adults in the modern world are suffering from. William Dement argues that failure to get adequate sleep is one of the leading causes of many health-related problems.

Sleep is one of our body's instinctive drives along with the drives for food, warmth, health, drink and sex. So it is absolutely critical for us to ensure that, as well as having more time for all the other areas of our life, we leave sufficient time for sleep. When we are well rested, we can more effectively work at our peak.

Sleep debt refers to the amount of sleep we are in need of at any one time. Most people are carrying around quite a significant sleep debt and this can cause many different problems, from weak immune systems to stress-related problems.

Often, we have such a scarcity mentality when it comes to time that we tend to believe we need to spend every second doing something productive. Sadly, we don't recognise sleep as being productive. It is always mentioned as being important but few people treat sleep as a priority.

It is essential that we take time to sleep properly so that we can be at our best for the time we are awake. This comes down to understanding our need for sleep and our biological clock. Here are some suggestions on working better with your body and improving how you sleep.

Sleep Better Technique

1 Find out how much sleep works for you. Some people can get by with six hours; other people seem to need nine. Find out what amount of sleep ensures you work at your best without leaving you with a sleep debt.

2 Do your best to get to sleep at around the same time each night. The key with sleeping is developing a pattern and this is true for adults as well as children.

3 Create an environment conducive to quality sleep. If you find yourself having trouble sleeping, ensure that your bedroom is dark at night with as few electrical applications as possible.

4 Avoid working or reading when in bed. Make sure you associate bed with just two things – making love or sleeping.

5   Work with your body clock. Once you understand how it works, take a siesta if that works for you and use your own natural rhythm in the best way you can.

6   Prioritise sleep as a very important part of your day, as you need to get quality sleep in order to perform at your best. Many people waste so much time because they are not performing as well as they can.

Exercise

Technique to Wake up at a Certain Time

Many people don't realise that they have a powerful way to programme their own mind to awaken at the time which best suits them.

1   Decide on what time you want to wake up.

2   See the time as if it was displayed on your clock and imagine yourself waking at that time, feeling good and alert, having slept really well.

3   Let yourself drift off on other thoughts and each time you think about waking up, imagine waking up as your clock turns that time.

Larks and Owls: Morning versus Night People

When we examine how we can improve our sleep and the best way we can use our biological clock, it is also interesting to note that there are some people who are naturally better in the morning and others who prefer the night-time, as that is when they are their best.

Those who find themselves sharper and better in the morning are often known as "**larks**" while those who fare better later in the evening have been described as "**owls**". Scientists have estimated that about 20 per cent of us fit into one of these two categories and the rest of us can be at our best at any time, depending on the specific circumstances.

Larks tend to wake up with a spring in their step. They find the mornings by far the most productive and can do the hardest work first thing. They usually leave the more mundane tasks until the afternoon and finally leave the mindless and easy tasks until the evening when they get tired.

Owls, on the other hand, are sluggish when it comes to getting out of bed. They are better starting with the automatic, easy and mundane tasks and tackling the challenging ones later in the day as the evening approaches.

Become aware of what times you are at your best and at your tiredest and arrange your schedule to work for you.

So, is it possible to change your natural style of preference? And why is it that most children seem like larks and most teenagers seem like owls? These are questions to which we are only now gaining intelligent

OWEN FITZPATRICK

answers. Researchers in the University of Surrey found a difference genetically between these two groups. As we have just seen, the appearance of daylight informs the SCN that it is time to awaken and this prepares our bodies for being up and alert. Our genes seem to determine how fast our clocks run and therefore whether or not we begin the day alert and raring to go and finish it exhausted, or whether we begin the day sluggishly and finish it with boundless energy.

You can certainly affect your natural style of alertness, but you cannot necessarily change it entirely. If, for example, you are a lark, you can minimise the amount of light you expose yourself to in the morning and maximise how much light you experience later in the day, which will help you set your clock a little bit further ahead in the day and will keep your energy levels up longer. If you are an owl, you can do the exact opposite. By giving yourself exposure to light earlier in the day, you can more likely set your body clock for earlier in the day and you will find yourself waking up more quickly and having more energy than normal in the first part of the day.

As for why most children function like larks while teenagers appear more like owls, the answer seems to come from the release of the chemical melatonin. As we've already seen, the SCN regulates the release of melatonin from the pineal gland every evening at around 9.00 or so. In babies, melatonin is released far more often, so they tend to sleep more, and in children it is released earlier than 9.00 p.m. In teenagers, on the other hand, melatonin is generally released around 11.00 p.m. This means that when they are supposed to be going to sleep, they actually feel fully alert.

Thus, we spend part of our lives in the lark phase and owl phase and only some of us seem to end up in one of these phases permanently. Although you can certainly affect these phases by resetting your body clock, perhaps the best way to work is to find out your body's natural style and do what you can to live in harmony with that style. Work to your strengths. The more you do, the more your clock will be in synch and you will reap the rewards of a well-timed body.

Dealing with Winter Mornings

Is your worst moment of the day the time you open your eyes in the morning? Do you ever find yourself hiding under the duvet, hoping, wishing, praying that you forgot it was actually Sunday morning and that your clock was two hours fast? Do you ever spend too many minutes trying to psych yourself up just to get to the shower without feeling the cold too much?

Well, if so you are suffering from winter morning-itis, which is a condition that I have just made up but have experienced all too often. Many of us find ourselves struggling in the morning, especially in the winter. So, let me share with you some strategies and advice that I believe will help you get the best from the morning and from yourself.

Studies have shown that one of the best times for sex is in the morning. It is also a terrific way for people to warm each other up and other research shows that we burn fat more effectively with exercise around this time. (This also suggests that the morning is a great time for exercise.) So the odds are stacked in your favour. Surely there is nothing more romantic than presenting your partner with a folder full of research suggesting that they will be better off physically, biologically and emotionally if they snuggle with you there and then?

Your body releases large amounts of testosterone or oestrogen at around 8.00 a.m. which makes this a good time to have sex.

Of course, this is not much help to those of us who are single, without the arms of a loved one to fall into. Instead, we face the daunting task of braving the cold, dark morning by ourselves.

We generally find winter mornings more difficult for two reasons. Firstly, the darkness of the morning influences our body clock, which is reset each day when it receives enough light. As we have seen, due to the influence of melatonin, our bodies are naturally designed to sleep when it is dark and wake when it is bright. Thus, we attempt to get out of bed when we are supposed to be fully asleep.

Secondly, the coldness of the winter mornings can make us wish to hide under the covers and wait until the day is well underway. Our body temperature already drops in the morning, which makes it easier for us to notice the cold first thing.

So, those are the reasons why winter mornings can seem especially challenging. Here are some ideas on how to beat the winter morning blues.

1 Set your timer for your heater to come on an hour before your desired waking point. Ensuring that it does will mean that you will have a nice warm room to help you get up first thing.

2 Have a shower soon after waking up. The stimulation of the water hitting your skin will soon have you feeling refreshed and awake.

3 Make sure that you have a bright light somewhere in your home. Turning this light on and experiencing it for a few minutes will at least help your body to figure out that it is time to be awake. Although artificial light is not nearly as powerful or effective as natural daylight, it will certainly help.

4 For the first hour, it is useful to have simple tasks which require as little concentration as possible, more automated behaviours.

5 Plan the mornings the evening before. Writing out a to-do list is a good start the night before so that you are clear on the tasks that you face each day. Also, it is a great help to write down what you need to bring with you when you leave the house and, even better, to place all those objects together where they can easily be found the next morning. It's also a handy idea to check out the weather forecast so you can decide what to wear and bring the following day.

6 Deal with the most challenging tasks an hour and a half after waking up. Most people are very sharp

at this stage and their concentration is excellent. (Of course, if you happen to be an owl, the reverse is true and you are better leaving these tasks until later in the day.)

7   Make sure you have something to look forward to in your day. If you can arrange your journey to work so that you are listening to your favourite morning radio show in the car, reading a new book on the Luas or tuning into your iPod on the bus, you will at least have the journey into work to look forward to.

8   Finding out how long the different activities of the morning take is another useful piece of information. Many people underestimate how long it takes them to get ready and therefore always find themselves rushing, leaving things behind and struggling to be where they need to be on time. To combat this, simply take some time to measure how long each of your routines take:

• How long do you take to shower, brush your teeth, get your hair and make-up sorted?

• How long do you take to eat your breakfast?

• If you exercise in the morning, how long does that take?

• How long is the journey into work?

Once you have added everything up, add 20 per cent of your average in order to account for the unexpected. Then you will have a good understanding of how much time to give yourself to get everything done.

9   As we've already seen, sleep is important. Give yourself enough sleep. Too much or not enough sleep isn't good for you. If you have to wake up early, you need to make sure you go to bed early.

10   Regular exercise is something you need to factor in at least three or four times a week, either first thing in the morning or in the early evening.

11   Getting a good breakfast and plenty of vitamins to start the day is another important aspect of starting the day right, as your immune system is at its most vulnerable first thing.

12   Remember the most important thing to bring with you – a positive attitude. Imagine the day going well and walk out the door with a smile on your face – and plenty of layers!

How to Defeat Jet Lag

When we take a trip across time zones and arrive at a destination where there is a change in the amount of light present for a particular time, we can experience "jet lag". Jet lag is an interruption of our circadian rhythms. This has repercussions. It is essential to work with this rhythm to allow our bodies to enjoy adequate periods of rest and activity. Working when we are supposed to be resting also disrupts the cycle and can lead to a kind of daily jet lag. Understanding how jet lag works is the key to beating it.

Try the following suggestions:

1 Prepare for the time change a few days in advance. Gradually change what time you go to bed, what time you eat meals, even change your watch if possible to reflect the new time zone.

2 Become aware of your body clock and when your period of clock-dependent alerting is at its peak. Identify what times it will be difficult for you to get asleep and use these times to do something.

3 Look after yourself during the flight. Avoid alcohol and coffee, drink plenty of water and stretch lots.

4 From the time you get onto the plane, adjust your watch and try to act in accordance with the new time zone immediately.

5 Upon arrival, walk on the carpet or ground in your bare feet to ground yourself.

6 Get outside into the sunlight in the morning as soon as possible after you arrive to help you reset your body clock.

7 If you are arriving at night-time, avoid naps on the plane. If you are arriving in the morning, try to sleep on the plane.

8 Before you travel, if you need to sleep on the plane, build up some sleep debt first to ensure that you are drowsy by the time of the flight.

9   Exercise upon arrival. Research shows that those who exercise deal more effectively with a shift in time zones.

10   Make it as easy as possible to sleep when you need to on the plane and upon arrival.

11   Give yourself some catch-up time when you arrive. Conventional wisdom suggests that for every hour of a time change, it takes you one day to catch up, although if you follow these guidelines you will probably find you adapt far more quickly.

12   Schedule your time abroad so that it works best for you. Anticipate potential times of the day where you will be more full of energy and plan things accordingly.

The Weekend Factor

Many people spend their weekdays working as hard as possible and then they attempt to catch up with everything on the weekends. No sooner have they caught up than they are back to square one. Welcome to the treadmill that is twenty-first-century life. For those lucky enough not to work at weekends, the weekend becomes the catch-up where they get the housework done properly, the shopping completed and can have a proper meal with their family.

It is absolutely essential that we don't let ourselves get caught up in this cycle. From putting into practice the skills you are learning in this book, you will find yourself having a different perspective on the weekends and how to use them.

Weekends can often be the time where we become run down and ill. When we are driving ourselves continuously to do so much during the week, as soon as we get a chance to slow down and take some time off, our bodies become more attuned to the symptoms that we have ignored because we have been so busy. Our brains and bodies have become addicted to action, information and a continuous need for speed, so when we have "time off", we find it very challenging to deal with. It can almost make us feel empty and we feel like we "should" be doing something. We need to get used to experiencing this feeling of emptiness and to embrace it. We also need to prepare ourselves for the time we have off by ensuring that we are getting good sleep, eating well and looking after our bodies, even when we are working hard.

One other quick piece of advice: when you are lying in bed on a Saturday or Sunday morning, make a conscious and deliberate choice either to sleep in or to get out of bed. If you decide to sleep in or simply stay in bed and rest, that is fine, but make sure you do it guilt–free, knowing that you are giving your body a much-needed and well-deserved rest. If you decide to get out of bed and start doing things, that is grand, but don't spend the time regretting it and feeling annoyed because you aren't in bed. Make the most of your decisions so that, if you are going to sleep in at the weekend, you enjoy it.

The Ultradian Rhythm: Our Natural Periods of Focus

The **ultradian rhythm** refers to the regular cycle of focus and wandering of attention that happens to us during the day. Every ninety minutes or so, it has been discovered that our brains and bodies cause us to drift away from whatever we are focusing on. This daydream state is very obvious to teachers. That may be one of the reasons why many classes and lessons are an hour long.

Many people struggle to stay focused and find their attention wandering, even when they are doing their very best to force themselves to stay on track. But since our brains are programmed to take this time to wander, it is important that we work with this rhythm. Once you notice your mind wandering, the key is to take a few minutes to allow it to wander and daydream wildly, instead of trying to force it to come back on track. This helps you use your natural rhythms in ways that maximise your periods of concentration. It is also essential for you to build in regular breaks every hour and a half or so to ensure you are using your brain at full capacity.

There is another challenge that we face, however, in our quest to grasp the fluid nature of time. Psychological time refers to the perception of time we hold in our mind, which is different to the outside "real" time. How we experience the speed of time passing and how we represent time to ourselves inside our heads reveals a lot of information on what we can do to improve how we use every moment more successfully

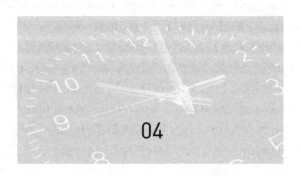

04

Secrets of Psychological Time

"Love a girl with all your heart and kiss her on the mouth: then time will stop and space will cease to exist."

ERWIN SCHRÖDINGER

Parkhead, Glasgow, Scotland
9.20 p.m., Wednesday, 28 November 2007

I was unaware of the cold winter breeze, which must have been blowing at that moment. The fleeting rain was barely noticeable as I turned my head and looked again at the clock on the scoreboard. I kept looking at it over and over, hoping that I could somehow slow time down. There were only a few minutes left and time seemed to be speeding along faster than ever. We still needed a goal. But time was running out.

It was the Champions League football match between Glasgow Celtic FC and Shakhtar Donetsk. I looked at the game and back at the scoreboard: 88 minutes and 20 seconds gone. Still one-all. We needed to win and we were on the attack again. But I looked back and the 90 minutes were up. We were into injury time. The referee decided we would play three minutes more and we attacked again . . . but time flew so quickly, I prayed as hard as I could.

Times like these are frustrating to say the least. Time seems to fly by. Yet a few matches earlier, when Celtic were winning against Benfica, time slowed to a lackadaisical crawl. Every minute seemed to take three hours to go by. I'm not exaggerating! Okay, maybe I am, but it did pass awfully slowly then and was soaring by awfully quickly now.

There is clear evidence that there is often a sharp difference between how we perceive time in different circumstances. Apparently, time remains constant in the outside world, but inside our minds we experience it very differently.

This is known as the difference between real and psychological time. Psychological time refers to our mental perception of time. Sometimes time seems to speed up and other times it seems to go slowly. The real time that passed at both games was 90 minutes plus whatever injury time the referee played. The time I experienced was far, far longer for the Benfica game and far, far shorter for the Donetsk game.

We've all had this experience. You're out somewhere enjoying yourself, and before you know it, your time is up. We have all heard the expression "Time flies when you're having fun". In contrast, we've all experienced what it's like to have to wait in a queue or be bored somewhere, where everything seems to drag along and time seems to expand to last forever.

Humans are not the only species who experience this **psychological time.** Other animals have different speeds with which they experience time, for various reasons. Flies, for example, need to process more information per second as they need to fly quickly and avoid obstacles; so, they perceive time as going more slowly. For us humans, a fly's perception of time would seem like slow motion. Flies only stay alive for a few days or a few weeks at a maximum. To a fly, a week can also feel like a lifetime – simply because it is!

Steve Taylor, in his excellent book *Making Time*, explains that there are certain laws of psychological time. He suggests that time slows down when we deal with new experiences and environments and when we are not absorbed in whatever we are doing or what is going on. Time speeds up whenever we are absorbed in experiences and as we get older. Also, the perceived speed of time changes depending on how much you want it to speed up or slow down. It almost works like Murphy's law (that brilliant Irish law that states "Whatever can go wrong, will go wrong"), in that whenever you want time to go slowly, it flies by far too quickly and whenever you want it to go fast, it moves frustratingly slowly.

Time goes by quickly when we are absorbed in experiences. It goes by slowly when we are thinking about the duration of such experiences.

One possible reason for this is the idea of comparative perception. All this means is that we think in our mind how we would like it to go and then we compare that speed with the reality. Of course, the reality is different so it feels as if reality is going too fast or too slow.

Psychological Time in the Brain

So, how does this work in the brain? Well, as we looked at earlier, as well as having a circadian rhythm, we also have an interval stopwatch mechanism that allows us to estimate reasonably accurately how much time has passed between two intervals.

This interval clock begins its work in an area of the brain known as the basal ganglia. The release of dopamine is the key factor in how we perceive time distortion. Dopamine is released in the basal ganglia, which records the amount of time that an activity takes. In future experiences, dopamine is again released at the start of this activity in an effort to measure it against the time it took originally.

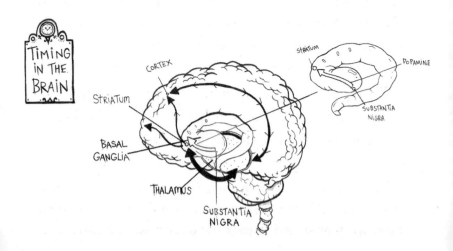

Since a function of dopamine is as a recorder on our interval timers, any lack of it in the brain leaves the timer running slow. When our interval timers are running slowly, time seems to go by very quickly and when our timers are running quickly, time seems to drift by slowly. So, the less dopamine available, the slower the timer works and the quicker time seems to pass.

Dopamine is a chemical released in our brain which is connected with rewards, pleasure and memory. We get a burst of dopamine when we get a reward for something or when we do something pleasurable. Making love, falling in love, laughing, dancing, shopping and watching football are all different contexts where many people get an abundance of dopamine.

For many people, getting a piece of work done or receiving an email or text message can produce a small amount of dopamine, which explains how these things can become addictive. Suffice it to say that dopamine is released and used up when we are enjoying ourselves and feeling good. The problem is, this leads to a lack of availability of it in the brain.

What this means is that when we are doing something we enjoy and that gives us kicks (probably one of the best expressions to describe the function of dopamine), our brain works differently than it does when we are stressed or not enjoying ourselves. It influences the availability of dopamine. When we are having a good time, we have less dopamine available, as it is already being released. Hence, our clocks run slowly and time speeds up.

Furthermore, cortisol, the hormone which is activated when we get stressed, makes the clock speed up and time slows down. This explains why when we are waiting or talking to someone boring or engaged in some activity we hate, it seems like it's going to last forever. Causing the interval timer to run quickly makes a stressful experience seem like it will last forever. Also, when a massive amount of dopamine is released, this can overload the timing system and time can seem to stand still. This explains why in periods of meditation and ecstasy, people often describe time as standing still.

So, is there a way for us to influence this neurological system through the way we think?

The Power of Time Distortion

Dr Richard Bandler, co-founder of Neuro-Linguistic Programming (NLP), has examined the way our thoughts create this "time distortion". He suggests that we can actually have control over this when we learn how to control our thoughts more effectively.

SECRET 1

We can alter how quickly or slowly time passes.

There are two particular techniques which you can use to control how quickly or how slowly you experience events. The first technique I want to take you through is how you can prepare for situations you might find yourself in so they pass more quickly or slowly as you so choose. The second technique provides you with a way of triggering the feeling of "fast time" or "slow time" when you are actually in the experience itself.

When you imagine an event in the future happening slowly and imagine experiencing it in vivid detail, like you do for events you look forward to, often you experience it happening far more quickly in reality.

On the other hand, when you imagine something as if it is going to fly by, you tend to experience it as seeming to last a lot longer. Your expectations cause you to distort how much time passes. When you expect something to go quickly it will usually make the event go more slowly and vice versa. The trick to doing this deliberately is to expect the situation to last a long time if you want it to fly by; and expect it to fly by if you want it to go slowly.

Exercise

The Speed Control Mindset

1 Think about something in the future for which you want the time to go by quickly.

2 Imagine, when it happens, time passing really slowly.

3 Notice how, when you experience the event, it will seem to go by more quickly.

4 Think about something in the future for which you want the time to go by slowly.

5 Imagine, when it happens, time passing really quickly.

6 Notice how, when you experience the event, it will seem to go by more slowly.

Again, this makes sense neurologically. The nervous system can't tell the difference between a real and a vividly imagined experience. Since you imagine something as going really slowly, you are setting the internal timer to go really fast, as little time seems to be elapsing. Then when you actually experience the event, in contrast, it will seem much shorter than you expected. So, when you deliberately do this, you will feel it lasting longer or shorter than you would expect.

Richard Bandler also suggests that when you recall certain incidents where you experienced time slowing down and you recreate the feeling associated with it, you can then associate that feeling with the experience for which you would *like* time to slow down. This works terrifically well. Once you learn to recreate the feeling of "slow time' by vividly remembering an experience where you felt it, you can associate that feeling with the party you are going to or any event you want to last longer.

In the same way, you can recreate the feeling of "fast time" and associate that feeling with doing your taxes or having that difficult conversation, so that time flies when you are *not* having fun!

Steve Taylor has also suggested various ways in which we can gain more control over how time seems to pass by deliberately becoming more or less conscious of our thoughts and more or less absorbed in our activities.

For example, when we let ourselves become completely absorbed in an activity, time seems to fly by; and when we become aware of our conscious thoughts, time can slow down. So, by becoming absorbed in what we are doing, we can more easily speed up time.

The interesting thing is that as soon as we become aware of the fleeting nature of time, that awareness helps time to slow down. This makes it easier to make things feel like they last longer than they do.

Exercise

How to Slow Time Down

Here are suggestions on how to slow time down for an upcoming experience.

1 Remember situations in the past where time went really slowly. Imagine it vividly.

2 Notice the feeling of "slow time" and, while feeling this feeling, imagine the situation you are about to experience. By doing this, you will link the feeling of slow time to this experience.

3 Become aware of the moments ticking down. Notice the time passing.

How to Speed Time Up

Here are suggestions on how to speed time up for an upcoming experience.

1 Remember situations in the past where time went really quickly. Imagine them vividly.

2   Notice the feeling of "fast time" and, while feeling this feeling, imagine the situation you are about to experience. By doing this, you will link the feeling of fast time to this experience.

3   Become absorbed in the activity. Avoid checking your watch.

When we get more control over our psychological time, we will be in a position to experience the events of our lives that really matter, more fully and completely. We will find it easier to stay in the present and experience life in ways that make us feel better. Time will be faster when we want it to fly by and it will slow right down when we want it to last forever.

Back in Parkhead, after two minutes of injury time had passed, I watched with complete anxiety and blind hope that something would happen in the final minute. For what seemed like the millionth time, the ball was crossed into the box and a shot found its way towards the goal. We scored. We got the goal we needed. Ecstasy and euphoric bedlam ensued. I found myself lifted up in the air as my arms were thrown around everyone close to me. We did it. And time stood still.

Timelines: How We Mentally Code Time

Another important factor in how we experience time is not just how we perceive it but how we actively represent it to ourselves in our mind.

SECRET 2

We can change the entire way we think about time by changing how we represent time in our minds visually.

When we think of the past, present and future, we have different spatial locations into which we place these three aspects of time. Dr Richard Bandler, using the technology of NLP, began to examine how these representations are organised into what we call "timelines".

Timelines are where we organise our representations of the different experiences and events of our lives. For example, when you think of the past, where do you think of it as being located? You might think of it as being behind you or you might feel as if it is to your left. You might find that the further in the past the event is, the further behind or to the left it is.

When you think of the future, maybe you represent it in front of you or to your right. When you think of the present, maybe you think about it being right in front of you or inside you. Everybody has a different way of representing time. People who generally put their past behind them, their present inside them and their future in front of them are referred to as being "in time". People who put their future in front of them to their right, their present directly in front of them and past in front of them to their left are known as being "through time".

In-Time

Through Time

Depending on how you represent time, you will have different perspectives on and habits around how you manage your time. For example, when you represent the past in front of you to your left, you are more likely to remember it than if you visualise it as being behind you. So, if you represent the past as being behind you, you are more likely to forget that you have seen a movie or forget various events from the past.

KEY POINT

Our timelines are subjective and everyone has a timeline which is unique to them.

Furthermore, how we see time is connected to our habitual patterns of punctuality. if you represent the future to your right and you think about Friday at 4.00 p.m. and Friday at 4.15 p.m., you can see a difference between those two times, as the gap between them is apparent. If, on the other hand, you represent the future as being in front of you, Friday at 4.00 p.m. and Friday at 4.15 p.m are much harder to tell apart, as the gap between them spatially seems more difficult to distinguish. What this means is that often people who are "in time" tend to be late, as they don't make such clear distinctions between times. Of course, this is not true in all cases, but it seems to be a pattern that is very common. You can establish this by asking people to think about different times in the past and future, getting them to point to where the image is located spatially for them. You can create a timeline by getting them to draw an imaginary line through the past, present and future experiences.

"In time" people tend to experience things more fully and with feeling because the present for them is inside them. Others, who sort "through time", tend to represent the present in front of them, and are less likely to experience things as vividly. However, they usually have a pretty good memory of events of their lives as they have the past laid out to their left in front of them.

Of course, there are different cultures that organise time differently inside their heads than we typically do. The Aymara tribe for example, represent the past in front of them and the future behind them, for they have "seen" the past, whereas they have no idea what lies in store in the future.

It's useful for you to know and be aware of your own timeline and how you organise time in your mind. Once you do, you will find yourself able to deal with it much more efficiently.

Time and Space are Relative

Our language is based and rooted in temporal terms. We have different tenses which we talk in. We might discuss our hopes and aspirations about the future; our regrets or memories of the past; or our feelings and experience of the present.

This importance of how we describe time must be taken into account when examining its psychology. We have developed spatial metaphors for time which have some variety in different cultures.

We all have heard the expressions: "I'll be there *before* one"; "I'll see you *around* six"; "Will you come there *after* lunch?"; "I'll be working on that project *up to* Tuesday."

When we use these phrases and others like: "*from* one time *to* another" or "a *long* time ago", we are talking about time as something which exists in locations.

Often, we describe events as being ahead of us or us "*moving forward*" into the future, or we talk about putting the past "*behind* us" and "*moving on*". It's fascinating to listen to how often we use these metaphors.

We discuss time as something that is moving towards or away from us: "That event is *coming up* soon"; "The project has been *set back* a few weeks".

We also refer to ourselves as travelling towards time: "I'm *nearly on* time"; "I'll *catch up*".

In cultures very different to ours, they have their own spatial positioning of time. Chinese Mandarin, for example, seems to organise time as going from down to up. It seems like our concept of time is interwoven with location metaphors.

So, why do we use these spatial words while talking about time? Well, the answer is that time and space are relative. We all think of time in a spatial way. What most people are aware of is that these words are effective ways of explaining time to people. What most people aren't aware of is how exactly this relates to the way we actually think.

Time Awareness: How we Experience Time

> ### SECRET 3
> **We change how we feel about and experience time.**

Do you find yourself getting caught up in the moment a lot, where you find yourself lost in time? Do you ever find that you completely lose track of time? Often, as we have already learned, this happens as a result of getting absorbed in an activity.

Some people, however, find themselves getting absorbed in the most basic of experiences. When they get distracted, their mind's focus is moved from one distraction to another. This kind of experience is also related to being "in time". It means that you find yourself existing in the present continuously.

Others are very conscious of time passing and are usually aware of what time it is. This is related to being "through time".

The crucial trick is ensuring that you are deliberately able to be either in time or through time in the various situations that each context requires. So, when you need to become more aware of the time that is passing, you can learn to go into a state of being through time. You can mentally change around your timeline so that it works for you. Here are some ways to do this:

Managing your Timeline

1 Find out how you represent the past, present and future. Mark out where each direction in time goes and draw an imaginary line from your past to your future.

2 Go back along this timeline and think about any positive memory and any useful learning you have received in the past that you want to remember and imagine placing all of those memories in front of you to your left so that they are easy to draw upon.

3 Imagine placing all negative memories and feelings that you want to forget far behind you so you can't see them any more.

4 Get used to switching between being fully in the present and being aware of the past, present and future. To go "in-time", simply notice what is going on around you in the present. To go "through-time", become aware of what you have been doing, what you are doing and what you will be doing.

Creating a Mental Schedule

Creating an effective mental schedule is something else that can prove very rewarding for you. Our mental schedule is the way in which we represent our diaries and dates inside our heads. When you learn how you best represent time, it can make it easier for you to store and retrieve tasks and activities in your mind with exact dates and times.

For example, in one episode of *Not Enough Hours*, I worked with a lady called Ann. She struggled to grasp the events that were taking place on different dates. Her ability to plan and schedule was not very effective. Indeed, her concept of the future timeframe was something she struggled with immensely.

When I talked to Ann, I discovered that when she talked about events in the past and possible events in the near future, her gestures were unusual. I found out that she actually represented events from left to right going into the future. Interestingly, she also framed each day a little higher as they went into the future and each day started at the bottom and moved up the different times.

This was fine, except that the standard way of scheduling time in the world didn't suit Ann, so she had to translate the different times into her own system. Her big challenge was fitting in with the world. My main suggestion to her was that, instead of her fitting in with the world, why not fit the world into her preferred way of scheduling? This really helped her and she was able to use her own fantastic way of thinking to master her mind.

Exercise

Create Your Own Mental Schedule

1 Establish your own timelines. Where do you represent the past, present and future?

2 Find out where you represent different points in the future. Check out the difference between tomorrow, the day after tomorrow, next week and next month.

3 When you think about any of these days, explore where you place different events that happen that day. Do they go in ascending or descending order?

4 Whenever you schedule something in, imagine placing it in the same location in which you represent the day it is on. For example, if you represent tomorrow a little to your left, place the

event for tomorrow in the same place. This will make it easier for you to remember it.

5 Also, ensure that you identify what time the event is on and again place it wherever you represent that time in your mind.

6 Check your mental schedule with your actual schedule every day for a couple of minutes to make sure you have it correct.

Your Philosophy of Time

It's important to remember that the way in which you think about time will determine how easily you will be able to handle it. If you perceive it to be an enemy, you will find it quite challenging to deal with. If, on the other hand, you see it as a welcome friend, you will be in a far better position to structure your daily schedule adequately and make the most of your time.

SECRET 4

The way you think about time will determine how you feel about it and whether or not you are under pressure.

The key is to make a real effort to become friends with time. The truth is, you are going to have to live with 24 hours a day, no matter what. It's like a goldfish being annoyed with being in a bowl. You have to make the most of what you have got. Therefore, the way you think about time will affect how well you work with it.

The question is, are you time phobic or time friendly, time stupid or time wise? Often, we reveal this in the way we speak about time.

Whenever people speak, they reveal how they think about time through the words they use. For example, we use time as something which can give value to something or not. When we say "I have no time for him" we are referring to the fact that we don't value someone's company. We are revealing that we don't enjoy the time we have spent around them.

The phrase "waste of time" is another interesting one. What we call a waste of time depends largely on how we interpret our experiences. To many people, watching football is a waste of time. To me, it is a wonderful use of my leisure time and gives me much enjoyment and satisfaction. Later on, we'll explore the various time-wasting activities that exist but ultimately, you are the one who decides what has wasted your time and what has not.

We talk about "doing time" when we speak of prison. We refer to "finding time" as if we have lost it. There is also a large financial metaphor used with time. We can invest time, save time, manage time, waste time, spend time and lose time as if it was a currency. In fact, we describe it as a currency . . . the currency of our life.

It's important to become more aware of how you talk about time because it will determine to a great extent how you handle it. Whatever expressions you use, become aware of how that expression affects how you think about time and start using expressions which encourage a positive and more useful perspective on it.

When we talk about time "running out", it is as if time is acting on its own in a negative way for us. Instead, it's more useful to see yourself as a master of your own time, in charge of where you spend it. This will allow you to feel in control, which will in turn make you feel far better about it. Studies have shown that as long as we are in control of our time, we don't mind being so busy as much. Furthermore, when you take active responsibility for how you are spending your time, you will find yourself far more satisfied with it.

When you describe what you are doing as "work", it can seem less enjoyable than if you describe it in a different way. Almost every person I know who seems extremely happy with what they do for a living has said to me, "I don't describe what I do as work as it's too much fun." We also have a tendency to refer to the old adage, "no pain, no gain", and buy into the misleading idea that change will be slow and painful and will take a long time. It is essential to challenge these concepts of how we describe time and change so that we have a smarter way of thinking about them.

SECRET 5

An essential key towards good time management is realising that you are in control over how you spend your time. Once you accept this, you will feel far more relaxed and in control over your life.

Once you have a better perspective of what time is, it is important to understand what your habitual patterns of using your time are. That way, you will learn how to survive the time crisis.

Exercise

Time Philosophy

1 Write down a description for what time is to you.

2 Draw a representation of time in terms of how you view it.

3 Examine both the words you have used and the representation you have drawn for time. Is it healthy? Is it positive?

4 If it isn't, examine what would be a more useful way of thinking about time? What are better metaphors you could use that would allow you feel a sense of control over your time? How can you draw time in a more friendly way?

5 Listen to the language you use when you talk about time and the activities you need to do. Ensure that you are talking in the same way that you want to think.

SECTION 2

SURVIVING THE TIME CRUNCH

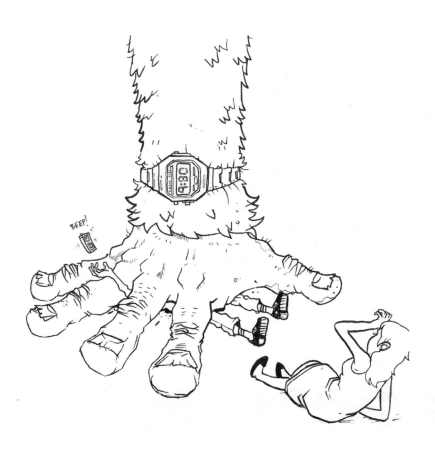

The Seven Time Victims

"Lost time is never found again."

BENJAMIN FRANKLIN

If you feel you have problems with time management, then you probably fit somewhere into one of the time types profiled in this section of the book. There are seven different personality tendencies, which I call the seven time victims. Beware of the term "victim", however. It is crucial that you begin to take responsibility to ensure that you are no longer a victim. Although you may feel like one, the following classifications are only tendencies.

I call them tendencies rather than personalities for a couple of reasons. Firstly, you can be more than one of these types at once. Secondly, just because you tend to behave in a particular way doesn't mean that is who you are. This book is designed to help you learn a system that will enable you to change how you tend to behave.

I firmly believe that you are not what you do; you are everything you can become at your best. To me, that means that when you change your behaviour and improve your life, you are simply living more up to your potential, which is who you truly are. The seven victims are:

- *The Workaholic*

- *The Perfectionist*

- *The Hesitator*

- *The Hurrier*

- *The Walkover*

- *The Time Stranger*

- *The Busy Bee*

These "victims" are not successful at managing their lives. They find themselves not having enough time or not managing their life and time well. Included in these profiles are simple and quick questionnaires to ascertain your time tendencies.

The key is not to spend time trying to figure out which one you are. Instead, it's about figuring out which tendencies best describe your approach to time and, most importantly, what you can do about it. I have used examples from some of the people that I worked with in the first series of Not Enough Hours, *whose characteristics quite accurately followed the characters of the time types.*

05

The Workaholic

"The reward for work well done is the opportunity to do more."

JONAS SALK

Workaholics are addicted to work. Work is constantly on their mind and even when they spend time with their family, work issues are constantly being processed at the back of their mind. A continuous need to keep working non-stop eats away at the workaholic. Any escape or holiday is short-lived as it can be more frustrating than they can stand.

This can be partly a good sign because often it indicates that they love their work and enjoy their job. The problem is not that they enjoy it but that it dominates their life. They fail to take appropriate time out to enjoy the other wonderful things going on in their life.

People who are workaholics will generally use excuses to make their overworking seem okay. They'll say things like, "I just have to get this job done and then I'll have time to unwind"; "This work has to be done now and it all depends on me doing it"; "I'll be no good to anyone unless my mind is clear and it won't be clear until I finish that project."

Workaholics also tend to find it hard to let go of responsibility. They take far too much on board and are very reluctant to delegate jobs to others. This sometimes involves a need for control and can suggest perfectionist tendencies, but not always. Their failure to let go of responsibility, however, means that they are unable to take a long break and a proper holiday is something of a fantasy for them.

Workaholics often work through lunch and late into the evening. They will regularly take work home with them and can be found, at all hours, doing invoices and checking emails.

The big problem is that when you spend all your time working, it is almost impossible for you to see the wood from the trees and recognise the implications for your family, friends and the rest of your life. You become so immersed in work that you know something isn't right but you are too stuck in the rut to know what to do about it.

In the 1800s, after the establishment of scientific management, employees were expected to work long hours, often for six-day weeks. The establishment of trade unions saw the fight for employee rights begin. Nowadays, many people work long hours and often seven-day weeks, not because they have to but because they choose to. Work has become something that many people feel the need to do most of the time.

There are some examples, however, of people rebelling against this need to work. Downshifting is the term given to a fairly new phenomenon where busy men and women decide to give up a well-paid job for a much less financially rewarding job in order to have more time to live a better, more relaxed and happier life.

You don't need to go this far to create balance in your life. One good example of a workaholic was Conor Holmes, who I worked with on the *Not Enough Hours* programme. It was obvious from the start that Conor was no stranger to hard work. Conor was a typical example of a "workaholic". He was addicted to the office and, every evening, would bring home his laptop and work away on it at every available opportunity. Whenever he was at home, he was also at work and his attention was usually split in a number of different directions. He worked more than 12 hours a day and had found himself putting in 20-hour days from time to time.

Setting up the "Outside the Box" educational publishing business was Conor's effort to actually reduce the amount of time he was working. Until then he had been working hard in a similar role for a foreign publisher. Because Conor had to go on many overseas trips, he made the decision to start his own company so he would have more time to spend with his family.

Unfortunately, this change in lifestyle actually led to Conor spending more time away from his wife Kate and their children. Having your own business at stake often motivates people to go above and beyond typical working hours. The knowledge that every minute you are not spending working means you aren't earning can encourage work obsession.

The issue with Conor was always about getting him to break his addiction to work. I had to get him to reach a threshold where he suddenly got a new perspective on work. He already wanted to change, which was evident from him applying to be a participant in the programme. The problem was that, he was so caught up in his work, he hadn't taken the time to really look at what he was missing out on.

Like many people out there, Conor was so determined to grow his business that his focus was tunnelled on work. One of the things I suggested he do was to acknowledge that every time he took on more work at the last minute when he was supposed to be spending quality time with his family, he was telling his family that they weren't as important as work. This was very hard for him to hear. Added to that, he began to see how his obsession with the office was affecting his relationship with his children, in particular his young son Ben. This was really the crisis point that provoked Conor into changing.

Exercise
Are You a Workaholic?

How many hours a week do you work?

40 hours	Normal Zone	1
50 hours	Hard Worker Zone	3
60 hours and above	Workaholic Zone	5

How often do you bring work home from the office?

Never	Normal Zone	1
Sometimes	Hard Worker Zone	3
Always	Workaholic Zone	5

How many days a week do you work on average?

3-5 days	Normal Zone	1
5-6 days	Hard Worker Zone	3
7 days	Workaholic Zone	5

Do you find yourself constantly thinking and talking about work in your time off?

Never	Normal Zone	1
Sometimes	Hard Worker Zone	3
Most of the time	Workaholic Zone	5

How often do you check your email?

Couple of Times a Day	Normal Zone	1
Every Hour	Hard Worker Zone	3
Every Few Minutes	Workaholic Zone	5

5–12: Normal
You work as much as you are supposed to. No more, possibly less.

13–18: Hard Worker
You work hard and do as well as you can.

19–25: Workaholic
Your life is the office. Time off – what's that?

Why are People Workaholics?

With the emergence of many new entrepreneurs, the continuous work ethic can mean that the more you work, the more money you earn. In this status-seeking, money driven culture, many people are forsaking quality time for a quantity of money. This drive towards financial reward encourages many to over-work.

There also an expectation in many different businesses to stay extra hours and do far more than is asked of you. The corporate culture often emphasises how important overtime is as a sign of a good worker. In such a culture, being seen in the office earlier than normal and later than normal suggests that you are doing your very best at your job. The reality can be very different, however, as often people who stay late aren't nearly as productive as those who leave on time.

Also, work can sometimes be an escape from the loneliness or emptiness of someone's personal life. Work is something certain that people can get lost in to avoid the uncomfortable reality that waits for them at home. That is why it is essential to build a balanced and happy life outside work while reducing the time you spend in the office.

How to Cure Your Addiction to Work

1 Take a good look at your life and ask yourself how important it is for you to be spending more quality time with your loved ones instead of working.

2 Master the art of switching off. When you leave work, consciously switch things off and get closure.

Mentally create a ritual to switch off (e.g. taking a shower, changing out of work clothes, etc.)

3   Schedule in your time-off as non-moveable time. You have to learn to prioritise quality time with yourself and your family as being at least as important as work time, if not more so.

4   Leave the laptop and work in the office. If you work from home, put the work away and discipline yourself only to go into the office when you officially start work.

5   Balance extra work with extra family time. The more you take on one day, the more time you take off at a later stage.

6   Use a to-do list to allow you to keep track of your work and focus your mind on getting things done. Doing a list for the next day each evening before you finish work should also help you to switch off.

7   Start a hobby which you enjoy and that you can improve on. Find something competitive to substitute for your work competitiveness.

8   Learn to identify the tasks that are urgent and important, which you will learn about in Chapter 14, "How to Prioritise".

9   Examine your business and ask yourself the question: what kind of changes can you implement that will make your job easier, better and more efficient? Start implementing these changes.

10 Ensure that you are delegating enough work to staff members.

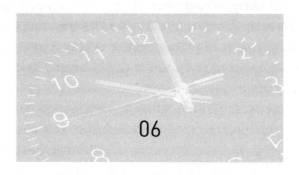

06

The Perfectionist

"The closest to perfection a person ever comes is when he fills out a job application form."

STANLEY J. RANDALL

Perfectionists are focused on making everything perfect. The house must be sparklingly clean, the food must be cooked as Jamie or Nigella would cook it, everything must be ideal. By obsessing so much about perfection, they can often waste valuable time that could be used for more important activities. Perfectionists also have a need for control and it can involve them taking on others' responsibilities in order for the tasks to be "done properly".

One good example of this from *Not Enough Hours* was Siobhan Devins. Siobhan had very high standards in terms of how she expected everything to be done. It was therefore challenging for her to let go of the reins of control to her husband Gerry, who was able to do the household chores very effectively. The object of the programme was for Siobhan to let go of control of the tasks she completed and to trust Gerry to do them instead. Gerry proved himself trustworthy and they had a blueprint of understanding to take with them into the future.

By setting unrealistically high standards for themselves, with lofty, unattainable goals, perfectionists are never satisfied and find themselves constantly frustrated. Marina Rosta from the series is another good example of this. Marina was losing touch with enjoying her life and was too busy trying to live up to her plan, doing everything the way she felt she "should" do it. She needed to learn to relax, have more fun and become more tolerant of things not being perfect.

Marina was used to doing things in the best possible way for the perfect outcome. Her obsessive cleaning, tidying and cooking displayed a need for her to be the perfect homemaker and mother. She knew, however, that in doing so she was missing out on quality time she could be spending with her sons and daughter. She had an amazing ability to ensure that the children ate very healthily. When I worked with Marina, my main aim was getting her to realise the importance of emotional nutrition as well as physical nutrition.

To do this, I took some examples from Marina's life. She would take a trip to the supermarket every day for fresh food; on the other hand, she was missing out on time spent reading bedtime stories to her daughter Saoirse and teaching piano to her son Liam. I provoked Marina by suggesting that she was prioritising the freshness of a head of lettuce over her children. This produced a strong reaction from her and allowed her to make progress much more easily in examining her true priorities. Sometimes that is what is needed to really remind someone what is most important.

Once she examined her priorities, Marina began to prioritise such quality time with the children over time she had previously spent obsessing about being perfect at everything.

I also worked with a lady in India who was a perfectionist. She was always disappointed with special events in her life because she imagined them going perfectly and they never went the way she imagined them. What she began to see, however, was that sometimes the best part of such events is when they deviate from the plan.

When things are not perfect, you are free to enjoy them a lot more, because you don't have some preordained standards to live up to or achieve. It is about understanding that the unexpected moments can improve our lives and be far better than the ones we class as perfect, because perfect moments do not exist.

Exercise

Are You a Perfectionist?

Do you find yourself spending long hours obsessively cleaning?

Never	Relaxed Zone	1
Sometimes	Effort Zone	3
Always	Perfectionist Zone	5

Do you have to do everything yourself to make sure it is done correctly?

Never	Relaxed Zone	1
Sometimes	Effort Zone	3
Always	Perfectionist Zone	5

Is it better to get something completed well or half done perfectly?

Done Reasonably Well	Relaxed Zone	1
Half Done Perfectly	Perfectionist Zone	5

Do you find yourself re-doing work you have delegated to someone else?

Never	Relaxed Zone	1
Sometimes	Effort Zone	3
Most of the time	Perfectionist Zone	5

Do you notice when something isn't done perfectly?

Never	Relaxed Zone	1
Sometimes	Effort Zone	3
Most of the time	Perfectionist Zone	5

5–12: Relaxed
You are relaxed about things and find it easy to let things be.

13–18: Effort
You make an effort to make things better than they are but can and do accept less than perfect standards.

19–25: Perfectionist
You feel a need for things to be perfect.

Why Are People Perfectionists?

Perfectionists feel a need to be perfect because they develop a belief that things should be done perfectly or not at all. They value perfection as something which is necessary rather than desired. The problem is that they often spend far too much time trying to achieve the impossible – complete perfection – at the expense of doing a good job.

It is good to have high standards. The problem arises when these standards are always higher than can be realistically or practically achieved. It is an all-or-nothing attitude. Perfectionists find themselves always disappointed because, as Dr Richard Bandler explains, "Disappointment requires adequate planning". They have set up so many ways to be disappointed and just one way to be happy: complete perfection. They need to learn to let go of needing this.

Many very successful people are perfectionists in different areas of their lives, which drives them to be brilliant at what they do. This is a good thing. The key is to ensure that your perfectionist tendency leads you towards more success and not wasted time and frustrated moments.

How to Let Go of the Need to Be Perfect

1 Accept the impossibility of perfection and strive to enjoy things more.

2 Take time to enjoy the process of the "journey" rather than the achievement of the "destination".

3 Ensure that you have some time where you simply enjoy yourself which is not just focused on improving things.

4 Practise making some mistakes deliberately to improve your tolerance for imperfection.

5 Delegate tasks to people around you who can do them. Accept that everyone has their way and that, as long as it gets done, there is no "right way". Ensure that the responsibilities are fully understood by the person to whom you delegate. If there is any extremely important difference in your styles, talk to the person helpfully and positively about it.

6 Ask the questions: *"What if it is not perfect?" "Who says it needs to be?"*

07

The Hesitator

"To teach how to live without certainty, and yet without being paralysed by hesitation, is perhaps the chief thing that philosophy in our age can do for those who study it."

BERTRAND RUSSELL

Hesitators are those who waste their time doing something other than what they need to be doing. Generally, people hesitate out of worry, laziness or uncertainty. When they worry, they spend their time fretting about the possibilities that exist if they engage in any action.

Hesitators often want to do something but procrastinate because they fear failure. Sometimes they are too lazy to take the action they need to take or are uncertain enough to pause before they complete a task. They over-think and are likely to be negatively impacted by "paralysis by analysis". They find themselves stuck by endless potential scenarios that they run through in their mind and they are unsure of what they are supposed to say or do.

Sometimes they waste time making excuses – for example, they need help from others or the right conditions before they get started and therefore they wait until they can get this help or until the conditions are just right.

People often hesitate because they value fun over the work they might need to do. The tasks they need to do are seen as challenging and they put them off. They reason that they can always do it later, that they have time. Meanwhile, as they escape from their responsibility, the time ticks down and they are soon left with a nearly impossible deadline and a hugely stressful amount of work to do.

Others develop a habit of wasting time, which leads to hesitation. People can get caught in a rut, get used to being lazy and comfortable because they don't have to encounter a fear of change that they may have.

Hesitators typically make excuses and fill up their time so that they don't have to make any big decisions. If they aren't taking action towards their goal, then they are safe, because they have ready-made excuses which can hide them from the possibility of not succeeding.

Take Michael Gallagher, for example. Michael played it safe for a number of years and avoided any steps that he knew logically would free up more time for him and give him better quality time in his life. He needed to overcome the hesitation and feel inspired to take action and make the decisions that would turn his life around.

In working with Michael, the key was to get him to realise that his worries were getting in his way. He began to see that his problem was not with time or money.

Rather, he had a problem with failing. Michael felt that if he failed, *he* would become a failure. What I wanted to show him was that failing just means you didn't get the result you wanted and it is not who you are as a person. Michael and I discussed his attitude towards failing in a sporting sense, helping him to see failure in an academic sense along the same terms. He explained how "you just come back again better the next time" which revealed his resilience. When he got to use that resilience for the rest of his life, he was liberated from his limitations.

Most hesitators, like Michael, develop effective strategies for worrying by asking the question: "What if?" For example, by asking "What if everything goes wrong?" and "What if I fail miserably?" they create mental scenarios which leave them feeling stressed and uncomfortable. These questions keep them stagnant in the middle of a decision for a long time, unable to move and select from their options.

I remember holding off doing work when I was in college. There seemed so much to do, I couldn't get started. I would find any and every distraction that I could and I got lost in a flurry of rationalisations. I made up hundreds of study timetables and cleaned my room from top to bottom. Meanwhile, the time ticked away and I was left with a mountain of work to do and little time in which to do it.

Exercise

Are You a Hesitator?

Do you find yourself spending long hours obsessively cleaning?

Never	Positive Zone	1
Occasionally	Normal Zone	3
Always	Hesitation Zone	5

Do you find yourself putting things off regularly?

Never	Positive Zone	1
Sometimes	Normal Zone	3
Always	Hesitation Zone	5

When you have an important task to do, what is your first thought?

This will go really well	Positive Zone	1
There are good things and challenges in this	Normal Zone	3
What if everything goes wrong?	Hesitation Zone	5

Do you find yourself having a very unproductive day?

Never	Positive Zone	1
Sometimes	Normal Zone	3
Always	Hesitation Zone	5

OWEN FITZPATRICK

Change is:

Great	Positive Zone	1
Interesting	Normal Zone	3
Scary	Hesitation Zone	5

5–12: Positive, Proactive Attitude
You are positive, relaxed and action-orientated.

13–18: Normal Attitude
You hesitate sometimes but get to things pretty quickly mostly.

19-25: Hesitator
You find yourself hesitating and worrying on a regular basis.

Why Do People Hesitate?
People hesitate for a number of reasons. Some do so because they are uncertain of what course of action to take. Some do so out of a worry or fear of failure. Some hesitate to avoid doing work out of laziness and some do so out of an erroneous belief that the longer you spend thinking about something, the better the action you take.

Uncertainty is one of the things that prevents people from taking action when they need to. Many people feel a deep need for certainty and find themselves unable to act until they have it. In the uncertain world we live in, this means many tasks are not accomplished because people are waiting for a feeling to arrive that rarely does.

Many people find themselves procrastinating as a result of their excessive worrying. They worry and fret about what

110

can go wrong if they make the decision or commit to the action. Their hesitation is an attempt to put off the inevitable and their failure to do something can usually lead to more problems than they are worried about.

Laziness is a factor for some people who hesitate. They can get wrapped up in distractions and interruptions deliberately because they want to avoid the task that they have to get done. Anything is better than following through with it, so they will find other things to occupy their time.

Many people equate a long amount of time contemplating something with making good decisions. They seem to think that the more time they spend on something, the smarter the decision will be. Unfortunately, this runs counter to what really happens. Progress generally depends on intelligent, quick decisions followed by decisive action.

In his book *Blink*, Malcolm Gladwell suggests that when we think a lot less and use our initial instincts, we are more likely to make better decisions. The less we think, it seems, the smarter we act. Unfortunately, many people tend to rehash the same thoughts over and over again inside their head without actually making any progress.

How to Stop Hesitating

1   Identify your options in terms of what you are thinking of doing.

2   Weigh up the strengths and weaknesses of each option and make a decision.

3   Get clear on your goals and values (you can learn how to do this in later chapters). Make sure your

goals are vivid and inspiring. Identify the steps you will need to take to achieve your goals and break them down into smaller steps so they seem more manageable.

4   Interrupt your negative thinking patterns. Be careful with how you use the word *but*. Always place the positive comment after "but". Instead of saying, "I think I can do well BUT I'm worried about failing", change it to say "I'm worried about failing BUT I think I can do well."

5   Use a Worry Book. Write down all your worries in a little notebook and plan to think about them at a specific time. By doing so, you free your mind up to think in a more useful way.

6   Practise using a positive attitude. Focus on what your strengths are and how good you can become.

7   Set yourself a time limit and practise the habit of making decisions and carrying out actions.

8   Get used to acting when you decide. Take some immediate action. Even practise taking small active steps to get your brain used to following through.

9   Reward every action that you take. Learn that taking action is a good thing, even when it isn't the perfect thing.

10 Tackle the difficult jobs first if that works for you, so that your tasks become easier as you continue.

11 You can also tackle the easy jobs first if that works better for you, making sure it's easy for you

to get started. Make a deal with yourself to do the task for fifteen minutes or so. Once you make this commitment, you will have started and when you have started, it is far easier to continue.

12 Learn how to deal with distractions and interruptions (see below).

Time Crime 1:
Distractions and Interruptions

Distractions and interruptions are among the most vicious of all time crimes. Picture it: you sit down to do a project. Two minutes later, the HR manager walks by your office and catches your eye. You chat to them for about ten minutes. Finally they leave and you get back to what you were doing.

Next thing you know, you are alerted to email from the sound on your computer. You read the email quickly and decide to answer it immediately. As you begin to answer it, two more emails flash up, so you read them before doing anything else. After you have read the second of the two, you are preparing yourself to respond to all three emails when you get a phone call. It's your daughter and she wants you to pick her up after dancing practice, as her friend's mother can't. Because you have the phone in your hand, you then start to listen to your messages. You have five messages and on the third message you suddenly remember that you still haven't followed through on that order for your daughter's birthday present. So, you look up the website which sells it. As you are browsing, you briefly check in with the RTÉ news website. You find yourself drawn to a story about American foreign policy. While reading that, some more questions come up, so you follow some of the links. Next thing, a colleague pops her head in the door and asks if you'd like to go for a quick coffee break. You say "Why not?" and follow her out the door.

Does any of that sound familiar? If so, you can see how a typical day like that can completely rob us of so much time. It really is amazing how much time we spend being interrupted and distracted. Often people tell me, "I don't know where the time goes." And often it comes down to the fact that they are allowing themselves to be taken off track on all sorts of other directions and tasks.

This also causes us to be more stressed, as we have started so many different projects that we find it difficult to finish everything. Our lives become an endless stream of unfinished mini-tasks, which can rob us of energy. Every time we are interrupted in something, our brain holds onto this feeling of incompleteness, which reminds us that there is something we have yet to do. The problem is that our brain doesn't always distinguish between something important that we have left to do and something irrelevant that we have left to do. In the previous example, not finishing reading the news is left as an open loop and it creates a niggling feeling that we have something to finish, putting it on an equal footing with the important tasks we must complete.

Also, it stacks up far more work for us to do. Let's take the previous example. In this scenario, we have left ten things unfinished. The project, three emails unanswered, the five phone messages not heard fully or dealt with and the present not sorted. Six of those are things that we need to finish at some point. The problem is that each time we get distracted, that is another task that we have to finish. From the time you start looking at the project to the time you go for coffee, you have actually got one functional task completed. You have agreed to collect your daughter from dancing practice. That's it, and that wasn't even something you had planned to do as part of your work.

The project isn't even started and your emails still require your attention and replies, the phone messages need checking and responding appropriately and the birthday present needs sorting. And this kind of experience continues to repeat itself until you find yourself at the end of the day with so many things still to do and very little accomplished.

Now is a good time to point out the difference between interruptions and distractions. Interruptions come from external sources, whereas distractions are more likely to come from internal sources.

Others can interrupt you, a phone can interrupt you, and an email can interrupt you. But you can't really interrupt yourself. You can get distracted, however. Your mind can wander.

For example, while researching for this book, I visited the BBC website to check a fact about time measurement. When I did so, my attention was grabbed by a video that described monkeys working in a restaurant in Japan. I clicked on the link and, to my amusement, I started watching a video of a restaurant that had trained monkeys to serve customers. It was fascinating. Meanwhile, I wasn't getting anything productive done.

This is an example of distractions (albeit rare for me these days). Sometimes they happen because our periods of focus are waning. Sometimes they happen because we get bored. Regardless, there are ways to deal with both distractions and interruptions effectively.

Exercise

How to Deal with Distractions and Interruptions

1 Set aside time in your day that is distraction- and interruption-free. Lock yourself away in a room. Turn off your email programme and phone and make sure nobody bothers you for that time.

2 If interrupted, immediately say, "Hang on one second" and write a note of what you were in the middle of. Only then should you turn your attention to the person. Once you have dealt with the interruption, turn back to the note you have written.

3 Become mindful of your activities, stay focused on what you are doing and understand why you are doing it.

4 Instead of seeing things as an interruption, see them as a switching of attention.

5 Become disciplined to stay on track with what you are focusing on despite anything else that happens.

6 Learn to switch off when you need to.

7 Look for the most interesting parts of what you are doing. Ask yourself what you are learning from what you are doing. Also reward yourself for activities or actions you complete. This can often help you to concentrate more effectively.

8 Set up a ritual before you go home in the evening or before you finish a task of picking up and putting down the phone, opening and closing every drawer you have used and switching on and off the computer. By closing the loops of every task you were engaged in, you are telling your brain to close down the activities – that they are finished.

How to Stop Worrying

Worry is a process that we evolved in order to protect ourselves. When we worry, we consider potential problems that may occur for us in the future. We are preparing ourselves to face the challenges ahead. The negative feeling ensures that these future issues have our attention. Worrying can become an ingrained habit and we need to understand the intention behind the worry before tackling the way in which we deal with it.

Here are some ideas to help you stop worrying:

1   Realise the intention behind the worry. What is it telling you? What must you become aware of?

2   Use a worry book. Write down your worries whenever you think of them.

3   Use worry time. Take ten minutes in the evening to worry about what you have written down in the worry book.

4   Ask yourself the questions: "What can I do?"; "What is the most useful thing to do about the problem?"

5   Pay attention to the language you use. Focus on using more positive and practical language when talking about challenges you face.

6   Always remember to imagine what might go right immediately after what might go wrong.

7   Blow your worries out of all proportion in your mind. Exaggerate the consequences of your behaviour in your mind and make them so over the top that they become ridiculous.

08

The Hurrier

*"I have been on a calendar but I have
never been on time."*

MARILYN MONROE

The Hurrier is always frazzled, running from one place to
the next, is rarely on time and finds that their life is
completely chaotic. Hurriers are sometimes lazy but
almost always scatty. They take on plenty but find
themselves getting things done at the last possible
moment, and sometimes *after* the last possible moment.

They are professional excuse-makers and will spend
an excessive amount of time creating and perfecting the
ideal excuse for their tardiness or scatterbrained
approach to their work. Often, they are late because they
themselves hate waiting. They like to arrive in the thick of
the action when things have already started.

This kind of attitude can be pretty self-centred. By
being late, they demonstrate that they are focused on

themselves and their own desire not to wait and don't seem to be paying attention to the feelings of others. They might not mean to seem arrogant but often come across like that. I remember when I used to be late, a friend of mine said to me sarcastically, "It's fine. I suppose your time *is* more important than mine." That hit me so hard in the gut that from then on things changed for me.

Latecomers are always rushing and never seem to make it on time. Olivia Lavelle, whom I worked with in the show, was not great at judging time and was late far too often. This resulted in her missing out on things and not being able to spend as much time as she wanted with her young son. She needed to learn how to become more punctual and arrive on time all the time so that she could make the most out of each day.

I helped Olivia become aware of how important it was for her to be on time and of how long her normal routine took. By learning this, Olivia was able to make a powerful change for herself. Initially, she had learned to think about her daily activities in terms of her best time ever. So, for everything she did, she estimated how long it would take based upon how long it took her once, years ago, when she managed to get it done ridiculously quickly. This superhuman mentality is not useful when estimating the length of time of an event.

There are many famous people who are late. Bill Clinton, for example, was known for his tardiness. We all know someone who is always late. Some of us are that person. Sooner or later, people realise the importance of being reliable and dependable and can make deliberate choices to make it on time. They are able to resist the urge

to pack extra tasks in. Hurrying causes many extra challenges that we face when we are always in a rush. It's essential to learn to slow down when we can.

Exercise
Are You a Hurrier?

Would your friends describe you as scatty?

Never	Organised Zone	1
Sometimes	Normal Zone	3
Always	Hurry Zone	5

Do you find yourself rushing around out of breath?

Never	Organised Zone	1
Sometimes	Normal Zone	3
Always	Hurry Zone	5

Do you ever miss important flights, trains or buses or the start of meetings?

Never	Organised Zone	1
Once or Twice Before	Normal Zone	3
Often	Hurry Zone	5

Do you ever forget things because you are in a rush?

Never	Organised Zone	1
Sometimes	Normal Zone	3
Always	Hurry Zone	5

Being early is:

Very Important	Organised Zone	1
Good	Normal Zone	3
Unimportant	Hurry Zone	5

5–12: Organised Attitude
You are organised and relaxed and never in a hurry.

13–18: Normal Attitude
You are only in a hurry from time to time and are reasonably organised.

19–25: Hurrier
You are always manically rushing about, disorganised and scatty.

Why Do People Hurry?

People hurry for a number of reasons. For some, it is the adrenalin buzz that they get as a result of being late. Whenever they are hurrying for something, there is an excitement there that they might be late, and the buzz or high they get from rushing about can be quite enticing. The feeling they get when they actually get there on time or not too late brings with it a chemical rush and a kick which makes them feel good. Why be early when we can get a good feeling when we are not?

Furthermore, a large part of being late comes from the need to be in control. When you are late, you are the one who determines when your interaction with others will start. It sets the frame for how you will relate to each other. Unfortunately, lateness has consequences in the minds of others. They may not say it then and there, but people register lateness and it can have serious results.

Other people are always in a hurry because they are exceptionally disorganised and all over the place. Through the habits they developed and mastered since they were younger, they have become poorly organised and find themselves rushing from place to place, often forgetting and losing important items.

Some people hurry because they try to do too much. They plan on what time they need to be there and they estimate how long it will take. This estimate is, more often than not, inaccurate and on top of that, they continue to take on more and more tasks to "fit in" before they set out for the meeting or flight.

How to Stop Hurrying

1 Explore the reasons why you have been late and address them. Does it stem from arrogance, self-absorption, a poor concept of time, need for control or trying to pack too much in? Make a conscious, deliberate decision to change for good.

2 Measure how long your daily activities take and add 20 per cent. Use this as a future estimate for how long they will take you.

3 Plan to be early and not just on time.

4 Learn to enjoy being early and explore the benefits of people-watching, getting some reading done or finding something else to do while you are waiting.

5 Become more organised. Start being more mindful over what you have to do and when you have to do it. Take some time each week to preview the next seven days.

6 Find ways to punish yourself if you are late. For example, agree with a friend that you will pay for dinner if you are even a minute late. Find ways of ensuring that there are always consequences to your lateness.

7 Learn to say "No" to those extra few tasks before you head out the door. Can you do them? Probably yes. Is it the best thing for you to try? Probably no.

8 List out all the reasons for you to change this habit in the future. Consider how it will impact the lives of others, make a bad impression, destroy your career prospects and all the other negative consequences it will have.

9 Find other ways to get the "rush" you used to get from hurrying about the place. Make being early by five minutes a contest for you. Make your new changes something you must maintain as a part of a game. Make the new behaviour more exciting than the old.

10 Slow down. Begin to prepare for the times when you normally rush and give yourself more time.

Begin to enjoy going more slowly. Give yourself time to think things through. Often your first instinct is excellent but it pays to have some time to figure out how to put your ideas into action. It also helps you relax far more.

09

The Walkover

"The art of leadership is saying no, not saying yes.
It is very easy to say yes."

Tony Blair

Walkovers cannot say "No". They find themselves taking on too much, mainly because whenever they are asked to do something they immediately comply. This means that they soon find themselves with far too much on their plate – most of it made up of things that other people asked them to do.

They agree to everything, often to the detriment of their own lives. There are a number of reasons why people find it impossible to say No, which we will get to later (see Chapter 15). What is interesting to note about walkovers is that they usually already have busy schedules. These schedules are simply added to by the demands of others who are, themselves, only too willing to delegate certain tasks to the walkover, who they know will say Yes.

One of the clients I worked with was Margaret Mulfehill, who owns a hairdressing salon. Margaret constantly took on more and more clients who asked for her, because of the fear of letting them down. In reality, by doing this, she was letting herself down. She needed to learn the importance of saying No to others and how to start saying Yes to herself. By teaching her why and how to do this, I could make sure she started putting herself first more of the time.

Walkovers find themselves with no time to do what they want to do. They are living their life to please others and, hopefully, from time to time please themselves as well. It is easy to get burnt out when you are trying to make everyone else happy.

Exercise

Are You a Walkover?

Do you take on too much responsibility?

Never	Strong Zone	1
Sometimes	Normal Zone	3
Always	Weak Zone	5

Do you find yourself taking on others' responsibilities for them?

Never	Strong Zone	1
Sometimes	Normal Zone	3
Always	Weak Zone	5

Do you find it difficult to say No?

Never	Strong Zone	1
Sometimes	Normal Zone	3
Always	Weak Zone	5

Do you ever miss your lunch or breakfast because you are taking on more work?

Never	Strong Zone	1
Sometimes	Normal Zone	3
Always	Weak Zone	5

Do you ever miss time for what you want because of what others want?

Never	Strong Zone	1
Sometimes	Normal Zone	3
Always	Weak Zone	5

5-12: Strong
You don't allow anyone to push you around.

13-18: Normal
You stand up for yourself mostly but can be pushed around as well.

19-25: Lacking in Strength
You allow people to walk over you and find it very difficult to say No.

Why Do People Let Others Walk on Them?

People generally allow others to walk on them for three main reasons. They feel a need to be liked by everyone; they are scared to say No; and they feel bad about themselves.

When people let others treat them like a doormat, often they are agreeable because they want others to like them. They do what others ask of them because they want the person to look favourably at them. The problem is that when you are a walkover, others actually disrespect you for it and see you as "easy" rather than "nice".

Many people who always agree to requests are scared to say No. They might miss out on an opportunity, or they might let people down and feel guilty as a result. Saying Yes means that they are promising to do their best. Unfortunately, it means that they are overburdening themselves most of the time.

When someone feels bad about themselves, they often allow others to dominate them because they don't have the courage or self-confidence to stand up to them. The biggest problem here is that the more you allow others to treat you like a doormat, the more you will be treated that way and the more that will reaffirm your low self-esteem.

How to Stop Being Walked on

To stop being walked upon, here are a few important suggestions.

1   Read and apply the entire chapter on "The Power of No" (Chapter 15).

2   Accept that not everyone will like you, regardless of what you do, so do whatever works best for you.

3   Once you have decided your priorities in the next section, stick to them.

4   Ask others for help. By turning the attention to them, you'll notice how sometimes they have no problem saying No and you respect them for it.

5   Practise being really good to yourself and treating yourself the way you deserve to be treated. Most people don't treat themselves well enough and it's crucial that you do so. When you do, you will start liking yourself more. Schedule in trips away, buy yourself presents and give yourself plenty of quality time doing what you love.

6   Whenever you say Yes, ask yourself what you are saying No to and say No to whatever it is deliberately and openly.

The Time Stranger

"The only reason for time is so that everything doesn't happen at once."

ALBERT EINSTEIN

Time strangers are rarer time types. A time stranger has a very poor judgement of time and always feels like they are running against the clock. They have trouble understanding how much time has passed between two intervals and time seems alien to them.

To them, time is a bitter enemy and the malicious clock is always ticking down, robbing them of minutes and forcing them into deadline after deadline. Time strangers rarely have an idea of what time it is and when they do, they feel excessively anxious about what they are supposed to be doing.

Time strangers have it even worse when they have responsibilities in a family. Organising life for one person

132

is infinitely easier than doing so for two or three or four people. Preparing every meal, giving lifts, helping with homework, not to mention providing continuous entertainment, education, love and support . . . it can seem nearly impossible to manage everything when you regularly feel outside of time.

Many time strangers have a phobia of planning and the mere thought of doing so sends them into a flurry of panic. The future seems alien and impossible to capture. It is hard to tell the difference between days of the week or dates in the year.

One time stranger I had the pleasure of working with was artist and mother Ann Mulrooney. Because she had a condition known as dyspraxia, Ann had a very poor sense of time. She found that time was a stressful enemy that she had only recently made a truce with. Ann needed to learn that time was actually her friend and needed to develop a system whereby she could handle time in a calm and confident manner.

She was found to have great challenges in dealing with time and organising schedules. I soon found out that Ann's main problem was that traditional and normal schedules were foreign to her. When it comes to developing a better relationship with time, the key is to learn how you sort time and ensure that you use this system to organise your schedule.

In Chapter 4, I explored the concept of timelines, which refers to how we spatially represent time to ourselves. To help Ann, I encouraged her to notice what method of spatially organising time she felt most comfortable with, and I had her build a timetable from that method. When I asked Ann where tomorrow was, she pointed in front of her. When I asked her about the following week, she pointed again in front of her but a little to the right and farther away from her.

She also organised the time for each event starting from the bottom up, which is the opposite way of doing it in most diaries. So for her, 9.00 a.m. was underneath 10.00 a.m. and so on. By getting Ann to use this way of thinking about her schedule, which was far more comfortable for her, she was able to relate more easily to what she had to do in the following week. This simple shift had a huge impact on Ann and she found it much easier to deal with time.

Time strangers don't get on with time because they aren't comfortable with how they represent it. The key is for them to learn how they can feel more comfortable in their perception of time.

Exercise

Are You a Time Stranger?

Do you find yourself regularly checking your watch because you are unaware of the time?

Rarely	Comfortable Zone	1
Sometimes	Normal Zone	3
Always	Uncomfortable Zone	5

Do you feel under pressure by the clock?

Rarely	Comfortable Zone	1
Sometimes	Normal Zone	3
Always	Uncomfortable Zone	5

Would you describe time as an enemy or as a friend?

A Friend	Comfortable Zone	1
Neither	Normal Zone	3
An Enemy	Uncomfortable Zone	5

Do you find it difficult to plan?

Never	Comfortable Zone	1
Sometimes	Normal Zone	3
Always	Uncomfortable Zone	5

Do you ever find yourself anxious about what time it is?

Rarely	Comfortable Zone	1
Sometimes	Normal Zone	3
Always	Uncomfortable Zone	5

5–12: Comfortable with Time
You are comfortable with time and find it easy to navigate your way through each day, week, month and year.

13–18: Normal
You are like most people seem to be. Time is all you have and sometimes it's great and sometimes it's stressful.

19–25: Uncomfortable with Time
Time is cruel to you and you hate it as a concept. You feel restricted and trapped by it.

Why Do People Find Time Hard to Deal with?

Generally people are time strangers because they have grown up with certain beliefs about time and experiences in time measurement and management. Of course, for conditions such as Ann's, there is more to it and it is largely a bi-product of the way her brain works.

Indeed, many artistic and creative types like Ann may find themselves struggling with the rigid structure of time. Similarly, different cultures have varying perspectives on time, so that is another factor which may contribute to our challenges with time.

Becoming skilled in organising and measuring time is something which anyone can accomplish, regardless of those inherited or learned challenges, as Ann demonstrated. By finding her own creative ways of handling time, she was able to take charge of her life and bring about the kind of results she wanted.

How to Feel Better about Time

1 Change your attitude towards time. The way you think about time will determine how you feel about it and may contribute to anxiety, which can make the way you think and feel about it even worse. By developing a healthier and more useful attitude, you will learn to deal with time more effectively.

2 Change your metaphor about time. Whichever metaphor you use – subconsciously seeing time as being a strange, scary, uncontrollable enemy versus it being a familiar, predictable friend who has

been with you always – is a key factor. Start to open yourself up to the idea of time being on your side.

3 Use alarm clocks. Sometimes when we get lost or absorbed in an activity, we find ourselves entering a flow state where time seems non-existent and we don't notice its passing. This is not a bad state to be in, as it allows us to perform effectively, but it is crucial that we learn to bring ourselves out of this state to deal with other pressing issues and deadlines. You can deal with this cleverly by setting up an alarm clock to go off after a certain period of time you give yourself to remind you of something else. You can thus allow yourself get absorbed in activities, knowing that you will be brought back safely to remember what else you need to do.

4 Keep clear lists of what you have to do and scan them regularly.

5 Keep track of your appointments and responsibilities on a regular basis.

6 Use a digital watch and get used to checking the time regularly.

7 Be disciplined and practise the new habits of organisation and planning that you learn.

8 Learn the skills of planning and organisation outlined later in the book.

9 Use Mind Maps and visual aids to help you remember things in a way that matches how you think. (You will learn more about Mind Maps in Chapter 16, "The Art of Organising".)

10 Get rid of anxiety. Richard Bandler created a technique for removing anxiety which works very effectively. It is called the Feeling Reversal.

Exercise
Feeling Reversal

1 Find out what the anxiety is trying to tell you. Usually anxiety is a signal to the body to pay attention to something.

2 Once you pay attention and deal with the situation, the next step is to remove the anxiety. You can do this powerfully by paying attention to where the feeling is.

3 Notice how the anxiety is moving and pay attention to the feeling itself. Imagine the feeling reversing itself and moving in the exact opposite direction to which it was going.

4 Allow yourself to imagine the feeling rushing down your feet and out your toes. Imagine it in your body but moving down your legs into your feet and then out of them.

5 While doing this, let your body imagine that it is completely relaxing and shaking off the feeling. When you do this a number of times, you will find yourself feeling a lot calmer.

11

The Busy Bee

"If ants are such busy workers, how come they find time to go to all those picnics?"

MARIE DRESSLER

Busy bees have a lot to do. Either due to the demands of a hectic career and personal life or their circumstances, they find themselves always busy or always having lots to do. In the modern world, many of us become busy bees. From entrepreneurs with families attempting to juggle the demands of running a business while being an active, involved family member, to working parents, from stay-at-home parents to students and commuters, busy bees are everywhere.

Busy bees seem to be the victims of the time crunch through no fault of their own. Regardless of this, the trick is not to concern themselves with whether or not they have fallen victim but instead to examine what they can do to turn things around.

Dara and Ray Keegan are an example of a typical couple in the modern world who fell victim to the challenges of their circumstances. They have two beautiful little twins, Rachel and Sophie. Dara and Ray both worked full time. They found themselves stuck in a rut, constantly busy and unable to figure out a way to have more time together. They just seemed to be caught on a treadmill, living every day as if it was the same, almost like a continuous Groundhog Day, with nothing progressing. This is something to which many parents and individuals can relate. Add to this the increased anxiety of the credit crunch, which is scaring us into spending more and more time working and trying to fit in everything we think we should.

It was important to give Dara and Ray a bird's-eye view of their life. I asked them to create a collage of photographs of the twins from the time they were born to the present day. This activity, coupled with them seeing where they were spending all their time, enabled them to make changes to their routine.

Busy bees need to learn to step back for a moment and examine their lives. It is important to look at what you are busy doing and making the things you do a choice rather than something you fall into. That way you will have control, or at least *feel* in control, of what you are busy doing.

Exercise

Are You a Busy Bee?

Would your friends describe you as busy?

Never	Relaxed Zone	1
Sometimes	Normal Zone	3
Always	Busy Zone	5

Do you find yourself complaining about no time off?

Never	Relaxed Zone	1
Sometimes	Normal Zone	3
Always	Busy Zone	5

Does every day seem the same?

Never	Relaxed Zone	1
Sometimes	Normal Zone	3
Always	Busy Zone	5

Do you ever try to multi-task?

Never	Relaxed Zone	1
Sometimes	Normal Zone	3
Always	Busy Zone	5

Being very busy is a sign of:

Taking on too much	Relaxed Zone	1
Normality	Normal Zone	3
Being Important	Busy Zone	5

5–12: Relaxed Attitude
You have plenty of time to yourself and you know how to take it easy.

13–18: Normal Attitude
You are like many people out there. You have plenty to do but you can get it done and still have some time for yourself.

19–25: Busy
You are caught in the busy trap and feel yourself always on the run from one thing to another and have no time to take stock of where you are.

Why Are People Busy?

People are busy for a number of reasons. Dara and Ray were busy because they got into a routine that they got lost in and found themselves following schedule after schedule, unable to examine their lives from the outside.

Many other people are busy because busyness is regarded as being a sign of importance and success. The busier you are, the better you are, it seems. Unfortunately, nothing could be further from the truth. Busyness often causes more problems than it is worth.

Others seek to be busy as a means of escape from boredom or loneliness. By being busy, they have little time to ponder and consider the parts of their lives they are unhappy with. They reason to themselves that as long as they are doing something, they are being productive Sadly, this form of escape will only last a certain period of time before busyness becomes burnout.

How to Stop Being so Busy

1 Learn to delegate. YOU do not need to do everything you are doing.

2 Learn to say No. You do not NEED to do everything you are doing.

3 Learn to defer. You do not need to do everything you are doing NOW.

4 Organise things more effectively. You will learn how to do this later in the book.

5 Prioritise what is important and do that. Sometimes you just have to focus on your priorities and avoid trapping yourself in job after job.

6 Schedule in quality, fun, relaxing time by yourself and with your loved ones. When it's actually scheduled in, it means you can actually be busy not being busy for a day or two.

7 Practise staying in the now. Spend some time appreciating the moment here and now, what you experience through your senses.

8 Accept that you will never do everything and focus on the most important priorities.

9 Estimate time frames and decide on deadlines more accurately.

10 Become aware of any time wasters that steal your time.

Time Crime 2: Time-Wasting

When we talk about something that we didn't enjoy and that we didn't see the purpose of, we refer to it as a "waste of time". One of the factors that becomes a big obstacle for people in how they try to use time is how they waste it.

Time-wasting happens in all contexts and usually it comes along with a whole host of excuses. We waste our time doing something and then we waste more time making up excuses about why the first waste of time is a valid use of time, when we know, deep down, that it isn't.

We allow ourselves to be distracted and we find our attention wandering to a million different tasks, except what we know we need to be focusing on. The opposite to time-wasting is being very productive with time. That means ensuring that the time you spend is "time well spent". It does not mean you have to bully yourself into doing things you don't want to be doing. Later on, I'll explain the keys to motivating yourself and how to become more disciplined with your use of time.

For now, though, let's look at the psychology of time wasting. Sometimes people waste time because they are lazy. Sometimes it is because they are hesitating instead of doing something. Sometimes it is because they are becoming addicted to doing something that isn't profoundly useful for them.

The following is a list of time-wasters. Of course, not all television is a time-waster. In order for something to be deemed a waste of time it should have no educational or developmental merit and little entertainment value. Watching certain soap operas or repetitively watching a news channel are examples of television time-wasting. We don't watch such programmes over and over again because they are good for us; rather, we have become addicted to them. Here are some examples of what can often be time wasters.

- Television
- DVDs
- Newspapers
- Internet
- Computer games
- Social networking sites
- Unnecessary phone calls
- Unnecessary meetings
- Unnecessary paperwork
- Rechecking email
- Idle chats/visitors
- Bad communication
- Waiting for something or someone
- Worrying

- Trying to have things perfect
- A slow computer
- Repeated trips to the shops
- Looking for keys and items lost
- Bad filing
- Traffic
- Travel
- Cancelled flights
- A long queue
- Inadequate planning
- Bad delegation
- Disorganisation
- Hesitation
- Being on hold.

Exercise

How to Stop Wasting Time

1 Identify what you waste your time doing.

2 What can you do to stop wasting this time?

3 Explore ways that you can make the most of this time.

4 Become more mindful of how you spend your time.

5   Make a list of your activities and make sure they all have a purpose. For every task, ask, "What is the point of this?"

6   Make a distinction between things that you do that you are addicted to and those you do that you enjoy and learn from.

7   Look for ways to streamline your activities so that you schedule those that go together or are in the same location back–to-back.

8   Learn the shortcuts for your computer programmes.

9   Prepare for times when you are waiting by bringing things to do.

10 Deal with human time wasters by controlling and choosing who to talk to and letting them know your expectations about punctuality. It's also important to ask clear questions and not allow them to get side-tracked onto less relevant topics.

In Conclusion . . .

As you can see, many of the solutions for overcoming the experience of being one of the seven time victims are to do with better organisation, prioritisation and building new habits. Sections 4 to 6 of the book will explore these three areas in far more detail. However, before doing that, we need to take a look, in Section 3, at what exactly your problem with time is.

SECTION 3

ANALYSE

12

How Do You Spend Your Time?

"Time is but the stream I go a-fishing in."

HENRY DAVID THOREAU

When I am first asked to work with someone to help them use their time in a more effective way, I figure out what they are doing with their hours and days when I meet them. I need to understand what their problems with time are and where they are presently spending their time. I also need to discover what they want to achieve and where they *want* to be spending their time.

In this chapter, we will explore how to analyse your present situation and what it is that you want to achieve as a result of reading this book. I call this process "Time Coaching".

Time Coaching

Time coaching is the process of helping you take control over the time you have. It involves learning how to go from where you are to where you want to be. There are a number of key questions that must be answered in order for you to start gaining more control over your time. These questions are:

- *What kind of schedule do you have?*
- *How much time do you spend doing what you do?*
- *How much time do you need to catch up?*
- *Where do you want to spend your time?*
- *When can you find time?*

Once you have answers to these questions, you will be in a better position to start to get to grips with time and make the most of your hours.

What Kind of Schedule Do You Have?

So, what is your schedule like? One of the things I do on most of the shows is to examine a typical week in the life of the person. I need to get a firm grasp on how they spend their time. Once I do this, I can explore with them how they can change things around and find more time available for the things that really matter.

During the first series, in working with people such as Marina, Dara and Ray, I analysed the amount of time they spent in each activity. Using clocks to graphically represent the time they spent in each situation pushed home the statistics in a more impactful way.

It became apparent where most of their time was being spent. This insight allowed them to understand the real importance of making a shift in their allocation of time. It allowed them to understand the difference between priorities and realities. It often turns out that what people say is their priority isn't what they are spending most of their time on in reality.

In order for you to analyse your own time in the most effective way, you can create these clocks yourself.

Exercise
Building Clocks

1 Firstly, you must figure out what kind of weeks you have. For many of us, each week can be different, depending on what activities or responsibilities come up. For example, some weeks you might travel for work and some you might work from home; or some weeks you will be home in the early evening and some you will be attending night classes. In my own life, I have four different kinds of weeks. Some weeks, I do training and coaching in Ireland. Some weeks I spend at home writing and doing research. On other weeks, I work on the TV programme and for some I am abroad teaching and training people in other countries. Which kind of week it is for me will determine how I will spend my time.

2 Once you have decided the different kind of weeks you have (no more than four), create a time log of where you spend time. The best time to do this is while you are experiencing each week – keep a time journal of how you are spending each hour.

3 Next, list the various categories that are most relevant for you in your life. These would include the following seven categories:

- **Partner**: Quality time spent with your significant other.

- **Children**: Quality time spent with your children.

- **Housework**: All activities required for managing of children, house, car, finances, post, errands, cooking, cleaning, tidying, chores, etc.

- **Self**: Time spent enjoying hobbies and/or improving self in some way, as well as time alone.

- **Social**: Quality time spent with friends or family or time spent dating if single.

- **Work**: Time spent working for an income.

- **Community**: Time spent doing something in the local area and community.

- **Sleep**: Time spent asleep.

4 Now, not all of these areas will be relevant for you and your circumstances. The trick is to examine the different kinds of weeks you have and establish how much time you are spending in each area. A great way to do this is to create some clocks.

5 Once you have time-logged your activities, divide the activities into the various categories and find out exactly how many hours you are spending per week per category. Next, divide that by seven to figure out how many that is per day. If you want, you can do

two different clocks, one set of clocks for the weekdays and one set of clocks for the weekends.

6   Next, draw the various clocks. The key is to split it into some of the following categories. If you have a partner and children, you can use seven clocks:

- Self
- Partner
- Children
- Housework (including all chores)
- Work
- Friends/Family
- Spirituality/Community

For example, if you spent four hours in one day on housework, your clock would look like this:

AMOUNT OF HOURS PER DAY HOUSEWORK

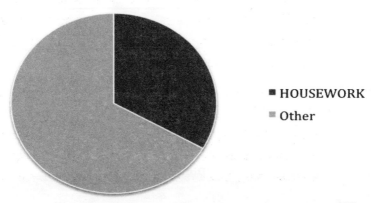

- HOUSEWORK
- Other

If you spend two hours in one day of quality time with your children, then this is the kind of clock you would have:

AMOUNT OF HOURS PER DAY CHILDREN

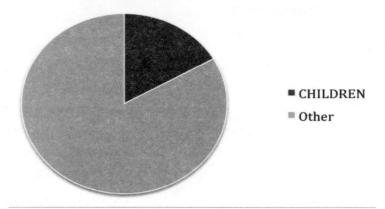

■ CHILDREN
■ Other

If you are single with children, you can use the following clocks:

- Self

- Social

- Children

- Housework (including all chores)

- Work

- Friends/Family

- Spirituality/Community

If you are single, you can use the following clocks:

- Self
- Social
- Housework (including all chores)
- Work
- Friends/Family
- Spirituality/Community

7   Once you have these clocks filled out, the next step is to examine each clock and determine where you wish to spend more time. For example, if you find yourself spending too much time at work and barely any time with your partner, you might want to look at that.

8   The next step is to find out how much of your time you are in control of. For most people, it is not the amount they have to do that makes them feel most under pressure; it is the lack of control that they have over their time that leads them to burnout. The key is to take ownership and control over your time.

9   So, examine your timetable and explore how much of your time you are in control of. It is important to remember why you are doing each of the actions in your timetable. Usually it's because the action is a priority or feels as if it's a priority. In the next section, we'll look at the difference between these two.

How Much Time Do You Spend Doing What You Do?

One of the important things to analyse and understand is how much time you take to do the various activities that you engage in on a day-to-day basis.

On one of the *Not Enough Hours* programmes, I had student Olivia measure the amount of time it took her from the time she awoke to the time she arrived at college. Her estimate was an hour less than how long it actually took her, which gave us a great clue about why she was late. The interesting thing was, when I measured her ability to measure time in the simple task of reading an article in a certain timeframe, she had no problems. She guessed the exact amount in seconds. When it came to an everyday activity, however, she performed very poorly.

Research suggests that people are often far more accurate in judging how long it will take someone else to do a task than they are at estimating how long it will take them to do the very same task. This is known as the Psychological Principle of Attribution.

Once Olivia realised how long it took her to perform each task, I gave her timers to use so that she could start planning and adhering to the set number of minutes each activity took. She got used to becoming more accurate in measuring time and, hence, she began to be early or on time for more events.

Often we make a fundamental error in our judgement of how long something takes us. When we include the distortion of psychological time, our perception of how much time has elapsed is influenced by a number of factors.

One of these factors is that, for actions we have done many times before, we tend to evaluate the amount of time it took based upon one example where we managed to accomplish it more quickly than ever. We look to the one time we managed to drive into town in twenty-five minutes and we seem to expect it to take us that long again.

It's vital that you begin to analyse how long the different activities you have in your life take so that you can get a fair and accurate understanding on how much time you have to play with and how you can best plan for your future.

When you know how long your activities take and when you add a buffer time of 20 per cent, you can make sure that you are always on time or early for events and simultaneously learn how to make the most of your time.

Deliberately become more conscious of how long you spend doing various tasks. The more aware you are about this, the more likely you are to become better at estimating how long tasks take.

Exercise
Time Your Life

Taking a full diary of your activities for a week or two is a great idea. Often people don't realise where they waste most of their time. By examining their everyday tasks and figuring out where they spend most of their time, it is often possible to help them find time where there seemed to be none available.

So, examine your average daily jobs and routines:

- How much time do you spend on the phone?

- How much time do you spend watching the TV?

- How much time do you spend taking a shower?

- How much time do you spend getting ready in the morning?

- How much time do you spend preparing and eating breakfast?

- How much time do you spend preparing dinner?

- How much time do you spend eating dinner?

- How much time do you spend travelling to work?

- How much time do you spend playing with the children?

- How much time do you spend talking to your partner?

- How much time do you spend exercising?

These questions should reveal to you what kind of time you are spending doing different activities. It may reveal that you are spending some time doing something unnecessary or it may reveal that you are using time productively, at least in those areas.

In work, you can also ask the following questions:

- How much time do you spend on the phone for work?
- How much time do you spend on the phone socially?
- How much time do you spend chatting at work?
- How much time do you spend on the current project?
- How much time do you spend at non-useful meetings?
- How much time do you spend at useful and productive meetings?
- How much time do you spend answering emails?
- How much time do you spend doing reports?
- How much time do you spend fire-fighting?
- How much time do you spend being interrupted?
- How much time do you spend on business trips?
- How much time do you spend on administration tasks?
- How much time do you spend on the web for work?
- How much time do you spend avoiding doing certain tasks?

There are three final questions to ask yourself:

- How much time do you have available in your personal life and in the office?

- How much are you enjoying the activities you are engaging in?

- What is the quality of the time you are spending in different areas like?

The answer to these three questions will make crystal clear where your time is going and in what areas you are spending most of your time. It will also help you discover how much of your time is quality time, valuable time. This needs to be dealt with as this is not just about how many hours you spend but what you do in those hours. (See "Time Wealth versus Time Value" below.) It's also a good idea to establish what you need to do to catch up.

How Much Time Do You Need to Catch Up?

You need to know what kind of a backlog of work there is that you have to catch up on. This can be done by making a list of all of the things that you have started but have not yet completed. Estimate how many days it would take you to clear the list if the only work you did was clearing it. You can do this by remembering how long similar activities have taken in the past.

As before, calculate how many hours this would take so that you have some idea how much time you need to allocate to catching up on things. Whatever figure you get, add 20 per cent as an extra buffer to make sure your figures are as accurate as possible. Then schedule it in.

Where Do You Want to Spend Your Time?

Analysing where you are spending your time gives you a great understanding of your present problems with time. Next, you need to be clear about where you *wish* to spend your time. You can decide which areas are the most important to you later. For now, you will become aware of the areas to which you just haven't been giving enough time in the present. We will expand on this in the next chapter.

When Can You Find Time?

One of the things I asked Michael Gallagher during the series was where he could find time. He replied earnestly that he hadn't found it yet. I then asked him if he had looked. He smiled and gently conceded that he hadn't. In fact, many of us are so caught up in the problems we feel we have that we don't take the opportunity to look for where we have time available. Analysing your time habits is a great way of finding this time. Again, more on this in the next chapter.

Time Wealth versus Time Value

As important as knowing how much time you are spending, wasting and using, it's key to know *how* you are using it. Quality time involves being able to enjoy rewarding time by yourself, with your partner, children, family or friends. It means that you are glad for how you are spending your time, as it corresponds with your priorities and the way in which you want to spend time engaging in your priorities.

Become aware of the quality of time you spend in the different areas of your life, not just the quantity!

For example, I worked with a businessman, Dermot, who spent, up to 14 hours a day, six days a week, working. He was a manager of a sales team and he was working hard to outperform all other sales teams. Meanwhile, he had a young family at home – a two-year-old son and four-year-old daughter. His heavy workload went on for months until his wife finally convinced him that something needed to be done. I helped him see how valuable and important time with his family was.

He made the changes in his schedule and started spending more time with them. Unfortunately, he was doing so by bringing his children to the office and having them play while he was working. He knew he should be spending *more* time with them, but he hadn't considered the quality of that time. I had to get him to see that bringing them to the office wasn't much better than going there by himself. He needed to enjoy his time with them and make it something they would enjoy as well.

When he eventually did take the appropriate time out to enjoy with his children, it was like a revelation to him. It allowed him to really enjoy the experience of being their father and watching them grow. This, he described to me, was priceless. It was real time value.

Why Do You Need to Change?

In order for you to make changes in your use of time, it is essential to reach the stage where you know that change is an absolute must. Many people know that they "should change" and they'd "like to" change but it is only when you make this change a must that you will ensure long-term change.

The mere process of observing how and where you spend your time will influence you to change it. As soon as you start to notice your time habits, they will start to change. The key is to change them in the right direction.

When you bought this book, maybe you were at a crisis point – what we know in psychology as a **threshold point**. If so, you knew that you simply couldn't handle the stress and frustration any more and you absolutely needed to change or the consequences would be disastrous.

Or perhaps when you bought this book, you were not at a crisis point and you simply considered that it might be useful to change. If so, it is crucial that you examine the true consequences of what will happen if you continue to squander and misuse your time as you have been doing.

The point of the clock-building exercise is to make you much more aware of how you are spending your time. Once you realise this, you need to see what this misuse of time will cause for you in your life. Here is a simple exercise to help you to do that.

Exercise

Ghost of Christmas Future

Answer the following questions:

1   Is the present use of your time damaging the quality of your relationship or your potential of having one?

2   Is the present use of your time damaging the quality of your relationship with your children or your potential of having children?

3   Is the present use of your time damaging the quality of your relationship with your family and friends?

4   Is the present use of your time damaging the quality of your health, fitness or wellbeing?

5   Is the present use of your time damaging the quality of your emotional health?

If you answer these questions honestly, then you will see some very valuable reasons to begin the process of change.

Now that you know your realities, you need to discover what your priorities are and see if they match. Before prioritising which activities are most important to you, it is useful to become aware of where you want to spend your time.

If you feel like there are not enough hours in your day, what are there not enough hours for? What would you like to be doing? In order to answer these questions, you need to learn to free your mind.

How to Free Your Mind

"When I let go of what I am, I become what I might be."

LAO TSU

In order to succeed in any area of life, as well as knowing where you are, you also need to know where you want to be. Most of us are so caught up in our problems that we forget to focus on what we actually want. One way to do this is to learn to free your mind.

Freeing your mind is about learning to set goals in the most productive and effective ways as well as developing the habit of writing things down to clear your mind of mental worries and clutter.

The law of attraction suggests that we attract what we think about. So, writing down your goals and thinking about them is in itself a powerful tool towards achieving them.

How to Find out What You Want

In order to find out what you want, the key is to explore all the areas of your life looking for the kinds of things that you enjoy. Freeing your mind will assist you in doing this.

So, how do you find out what you want? Well, the trick to this is very simple. Ask yourself the following questions:

Exercise

Find Out What You Want

- What are the things that you enjoy in your life at the moment and that you want more of?

- What are the things that you hate in your life at the moment and what are the opposite things to these?

- What kind of lifestyle appeals to you and why?

- What in your life don't you have that you would like to have?

Answering these questions should inspire in you lots of ideas on what it is you want to have and do in your life. Then it is simply a case of deciding which are the most achievable and desirable for you.

How to Set Goals

Goal setting is something we all do to some extent. In order for us to change the channel on the remote, we must have a goal of changing the channel; we then take action and move our fingers and – hey presto! – the channel is changed. Of course, when we talk about goal-setting in terms of improving the quality of our lives, we are talking about bigger and better goals that will make more of an impact on our futures.

We need to make sure we create lots of goals and evaluate which of these goals are the most important. Keeping an eye on the most important goals we set is the best way of ensuring we are living the lives we desire.

Setting goals is an art form. It is something that you can improve on. By improving I mean that you ensure that you are more likely to achieve your outcomes as a result of setting them in the most effective way possible. When you set an outcome or goal, it is important that you fulfil certain criteria in order for you to make significant progress towards achieving that goal.

So, to start with, what kind of life do you want? Really? What do you want to achieve during this process? What will saving time do for you? How will it change things? What do you want to be spending your time on? There are five aspects to these goals that must be considered.

Make sure your goals are positively framed, specific, sensory-based, ecological and under your control.

Positive

It is crucial that you focus on what you *do* want rather than what you don't want. Your brain will tend to draw you towards what it focuses on, so ensure that you focus on what you want to achieve. So, instead of saying you don't want to waste any more time worrying, it's better to say that you *do* want to spend more time feeling excited about the future.

Specific

You need to make sure that your goal is specific, with a determined deadline. This doesn't mean you have to stay rigid. You can adapt and be flexible as you move towards the deadline. It is important, however, that you give your brain specific instructions as to when, where and what you are going to achieve. It's not about saying, "I want a new place to live"; rather, say "I want a new three-bedroom house near Dublin, a mile or two away from the sea, and I want to move into it in the next two years."

Sensory Based

As well as being specific, you must also think of your goal in sensory-based terms. You need to imagine what you will see, hear and feel once you have successfully achieved it. This does two things. Firstly, it ensures that you have criteria that will let you know when you have successfully achieved the outcome. Secondly, by imagining it in such vivid detail, it can enhance the motivation you feel when you think about doing it.

Ecological

Your goals need to be ecological as well. By ecological, I simply mean that they need to fit in with the rest of your life. Often, people don't fully think through the consequences of their goals. When you decide to work towards a certain goal, it will require you putting time into achieving that goal. That time is time that is not spent somewhere else. So, for every goal you achieve, there are consequences. You have to make sure that the achievement of the goal is worth it, even when you take into consideration what the consequences are.

When you achieve the goal, how will that impact your life in the short, medium and long term? As a result of being successful with this goal, what are you going to have to sacrifice or what will you not have time for any more? What kind of person will you become when you have accomplished this goal? Answering questions like these forces you to examine whether or not the goal itself is worth achieving. If it isn't worth achieving, it is important to find out what is and adapt your goal so that it becomes something that benefits you and those around you.

Control

Finally, the goals and outcomes you attempt to achieve must be under your control or influence. It is pointless having a goal if you cannot affect the outcome. Instead, ensure that you have as much control as possible over it and if you cannot fully control it then become aware of how much you can influence it happening.

Every goal you set should be brought through each of these five criteria. To summarise, the relevant questions would be as follows:

Exercise
Well-Formed Goals

- What do you want?

- What do you want specifically?

- How will you know when you have achieved it? What will you be able to see, hear and feel?

- Is it worth it? What are the good and bad points in terms of impact on your life?

- Is it under your control or influence?

Let's have a look at some questions you can answer which will help you get more clarity on what you want. They are divided into different areas of your life.

Designing Your Life

- *Physical*

  ○ What kind of body do you want to have?
  ○ How fit do you want to be?
  ○ How do you want to feel physically?

- What weight would you like to be?
- How healthy do you want to be?
- What do you want to be eating and drinking?
- How do you want to look?

- *Mental*
  - What do you want to know?
  - What do you want to be able to do?
  - What expertise do you want to have?

- *Emotional*
  - How do you want to feel?
  - How do you want to deal with stress or challenges?

- *Social*
  - What kind of social life do you want to have?
  - What kind of friends do you want?
  - How often do you want to see your friends?
  - What kind of friend do you want to be?

- *Occupational*
  - What kind of work do you want to do every day?
  - What kind of worker do you want to be?
  - How do you want to get on with your colleagues?
  - How do you want to challenge yourself?

- *Financial*
  - How much do you want to earn per year?
  - How much money do you want to have in the bank?

- *Familial*
  - What sort of family life do you want to have?
  - How often do you want to see your family?
  - What kind of family member do you want to be?

- *Intimate*
  - If you are single, what kind of person do you want to meet?
  - If you are in a relationship, how do you want your relationship to grow and improve?
  - What kind of partner do you want to be?
  - What kind of life do you want to have?
  - Who will be affected by you achieving this life?
  - How will they be affected?
  - Will the change be worth it?

The Life List

The "life list" is what I call your lofty, lifetime goals. What are all the things you would like to do in the world? On the life list you can be free to write down every aspiration or goal you have ever thought about.

Now the trick with this list is that it is not about achieving these goals and it is especially not about stupidly feeling bad about not having achieved them. It is about letting your creativity flow and letting your mind roam free in the world of daydreams.

No matter how ridiculous, start jotting down all of the wonderful ideas you have about what you would love to do.

Whether it is parachute-jumping in New Zealand, climbing Mount Everest, driving a Ferrari, visiting the Great Pyramids of Giza in Egypt . . . whatever it is, write it down.

This is your opportunity to let your mind open up fully to all the dreams that you have in your life. There is to be no holding back when you write out your life list. Take a few sheets of paper and start writing down everything that you can about what your ideal life goals might be. They can be as lofty as you choose. The key is to let your brain unlock its imagination and creativity.

Allow your mind to dream wildly with the life list. It allows you to liberate your mind into exploring different areas of your life and this will help you become clearer about what you want in your life.

Exercise
Wildest Dreams

Answer the following questions and compile your life list. As already mentioned, write down every aspiration, no matter how seemingly impossible.

- What would you do if you had a year left to live?
- What would you do if you were a millionaire and had all the money you needed?
- What would you do if you never had to work again?
- What would you do if you knew you couldn't fail?

- What would you do if you could live forever?

- What would you do if you could stop time whenever you wanted to?

- Where would you travel to if you could go there in a heartbeat?

- When and where would you visit if you could travel through time?

Answering these questions will help you establish what are the things that matter most to you. While you might not be able to achieve some of the items on the list, they will give you clues into what excites you and will help you to be clearer about your more achievable goals.

The Power of Writing Lists

Perhaps one of the most important tasks that you can do to take control over your life is to write things down. Whether you use a computer, iPhone, Blackberry or pen and notebook, the key is to get into the habit of taking notes of whatever you have to do.

Get into the habit of writing a list in a notebook or journal. This allows you to become clear on what you have to do as well as freeing your mind of unnecessary worries.

Take "to-do" lists, for example. To-do lists have a number of functions. Firstly, they give you a valuable way of examining the necessary actions you have in a day or a week so you don't have to hold them in your head for any length of time. Secondly, you can start prioritising them by playing around with the list and changing the order in which you list them. Thirdly, to-do lists allow you to organise your day more efficiently by making it clear what different activities are on and what sequence you can best do them in.

The first function of to-do lists – to get things out of your head and onto paper – is the most essential. We all have "internal" memory and "external" memory. "Internal" memory refers to our own mind and the memory we have inside our heads. "External" memory is the places in our environment where we store information, such as computers and notebooks.

When you store information on your computer or on paper instead of inside your head, you free up space for your head to think more productively and effectively. A great way to start doing this is by engaging in the brain dump.

The Brain Dump

A **brain dump** is exactly what it sounds like. You literally dump all the activities and things you have to do or think about in the foreseeable future onto paper or into a document on your computer. This is a powerful technique to "declutter your mind" and get your brain freed up to think in the most useful, practical and smartest of ways.

The brain dump should include everything from business projects to personal matters. Everything and anything should be included and that may mean that it takes quite a while. It also includes the actions you need to take in order to achieve your goals. As well as writing each topic or task down, note beside it the timeframe involved: is it *immediate* (this week), *short term* (this month), *medium term* (this year) or *long term* (over the next few years)? Also note if it is *once-off* or *regular* (every week or month) or *semi-regular* (once every few months).

Once you have performed your brain dump, give yourself some time before assuming that is your list. Your brain dump can be added to and items taken off anytime you like. The key is that everything should be kept on this list until you are fully sure it is no longer something in your life.

It's important to be aware why the brain dump is such a useful exercise. Just like the worry book, the process of taking the things on your mind and putting them in external memory ensures that you can free up space to use your brain on other matters.

Exercise

Brain Dump

1 Write down every single activity or task you have to remember to do in your life over the course of the next year.

2 Divide them into the various categories of immediate (this week), short term (in the next three months), long term (over the next year).

3 Establish whether they are once-off, regular or semi-regular.

4 Add to this list as necessary over time.

5 Never expect to get it all done.

"To-Do" List

Once you have completed the brain dump, the next step is to create a to-do list. This is about taking the main things that you have to remember to do over the next few months and outlining them in a list. This should include everything that you need reminding on.

To create a to-do list, decide what actions need to be taken and how to keep track of them. When you fill in a to-do list, it allows you to get focused on what you need to do. You can also create a priority list, which is a list of tasks that absolutely have to be done. These are lists that you don't add to and are easy to clear. Once you learn how to prioritise, you can create your very own priority list.

Exercise

To-Do-List

1   Go through your brain dump and highlight all the things you have to do in the next month or so.

2   Identify any deadlines coming up in the next three months and what actions you need to be taking in the next month for them.

3   Examine all your goals and desired dates of achievement for them and figure out what actions you need to take in the next month towards achieving them.

4   Estimate what other tasks or actions you may be asked to do in the next thirty days.

5   Once you compile these actions together, figure out what sequence they must be done in. This is the order in terms of when they must be completed by and not according to importance or urgency. For example, certain tasks cannot be done until other tasks are completed first.

6   You should have a list of tasks to do in some kind of order that you can examine more closely and prioritise. This list can be added to and items marked off it.

SECTION 4

PRIORITISE

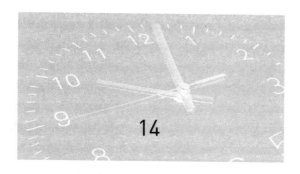

14

How to Prioritise

"Things that matter most must never be at the mercy of things that matter least."

JOHANN WOLFGANG VAN GOETHE

Anna was a 35-year-old IT technician and came to see me because she had no idea what she wanted. She was getting tired of her job and wanted a change but wasn't sure what kind of change. She found herself continuously worried about the future and was scared to quit her job in case she found something worse. Having bought a house by herself three years earlier, she had the responsibility of a mortgage. She described herself as being constantly "muddled" about everything and felt the world was on her shoulders.

Many people can relate to Anna. We live in a world with so many things we can do, it can be hard to figure out what are our best choices. Our abundance of options can make it feel like we should be getting all our decisions right or we will miss out. We can feel like we will be making a disastrous mistake if we don't make the perfect choice. Meanwhile, we carry around with us worries about the future and how our lives are going to turn out. So, we feel stressed and anxious and we suffer as a result.

When I worked with Anna, my focus was on helping her establish what things were most important to her. I wanted to help her free her mind to reveal what were her most important values. When she became aware of her values, it helped her figure out her goals and her priorities. She was able to put on paper what she thought inside her head and with that came a clearer understanding of the choices that lay in front of her. She learned to design her life and let go of the stress and worry about the future. This helped her to master the skill of prioritising.

Why Prioritise?

The question is, why bother prioiritising your activities on an everyday basis? If you have 20 things to do, what does it matter which activities you get done first? It is still important to get them all done. Well, there are two important answers to this question.

To start with, in reality, we are more likely to complete whatever we choose to do first than what we leave towards the end of the day. We need to ensure therefore that what we do schedule in for the initial activities of the day are the most important factors to us.

Secondly, priorities should be focused on, not just because they are the most important tasks but also because they are the tasks that produce most of our results. To understand what I mean by this, let's look at what is known as the Pareto Principle or the 80/20 rule.

The Pareto Principle

The **80/20 rule** was first described by Vilfredo Pareto in 1897 and became known as the Pareto Principle. Pareto discovered in one of his studies that 80 per cent of the wealth was owned by 20 per cent of the population. He soon found this kind of pattern replicated in a number of other studies he conducted worldwide.

In essence, this law argues that 20 per cent of effort yields 80 per cent of results. What this means is that it is possible to maximise productivity when you can discover what that 20 per cent is. The law also suggests that 80 per cent of the effort brings about only 20 per cent of the results. It becomes obvious that the key is to learn to prioritise so that you can spend more time engaging in the 20 per cent that is most productive.

Now, this does not mean that it has to be exactly 20 per cent. The figure is an estimate. The importance of this percentage is that it indicates that a smaller group of behaviours create the greatest results, therefore it is essential to spend more time on those specific behaviours.

If we can find the 20 per cent of what we do that produces 80 per cent of what we achieve, then we can focus more on that 20 per cent and do our best to improve our productivity and efficiency as a result.

So, how do you find out what 20 per cent of your effort is the most productive? Well, the first thing to do is to examine all the different tasks or activities that we have outlined on our to-do list and examine what each of them will lead to. This begins the process of prioritising by giving us some basic understandings of the most important behaviours we engage in.

Pareto Exercise

1 Look through all of your daily activities for your job. List out your responsibilities and the tasks you complete.

2 Describe the results you achieve in your business and identify which of the responsibilities and tasks you engage in that lead to most of the results.

3 Ask yourself how can you start to focus more on these tasks.

Finding Your Values: Your Code to Life

It's essential to establish what your values are. This will let you know which of your goals are priorities and it will make it easy for you to decide which tasks to complete first. Often, we need to identify which tasks contribute to our goals and which don't. This helps us to decide how important the tasks are or not.

Priorities can be defined as being the activities and actions that are deemed as being the most important to do. Values refer to the things in our life we believe are most important. Whereas values are associated more with general life, priorities are more specifically connected with the daily, weekly or monthly activities that we have.

Our goals often indicate what our values are. The reason why we achieve our goals is to satisfy such values. So, to begin to understand what your values are, you need to take a look at the goals you have set and ask yourself what feelings you will get as a result of achieving those goals.

Prioritising involves asking the question: Why am I doing this? The answer to this question will reveal whether or not the action results in satisfying your values. Priorities are selected based upon how valuable the tasks are in terms of helping us achieve our goals.

I describe two types of values: achievement values and personal code values.

Achievement Values

Achievement values are the values that are attached to achieving your goals. Whatever feelings you will get as a result of achieving your goals are your achievement values.

For example, if your goal is to buy a house, it is the feelings of security and freedom that you will get as a result of having the house that are your achievement values.

The way to discover your achievement values is to take a look at your goals and ask yourself the question: "When I achieve my goals, what feelings will they give me and which of these feelings are the most important?"

Personal Code Values

Personal code values refer to the standards that we regard as being most important in order for us to live our lives. We value things like honesty, integrity and truthfulness as part of our personal code.

In the different roles we play in our lives, we value certain qualities as being more important than others. To discover what these qualities are, the question to ask yourself is, "What qualities do I aim to personify?"

In order to best understand how we should prioritise our actions, it is useful to know what our life values are. When you are clearer about what is most important to you in life, you can more easily determine what to set as priorities and in what order.

Exercise

Values Check

1 Go through seven different goals you have in different areas of your life. Write down the feelings that you will have when you have successfully achieved each of the goals. Make a list of these feelings.

2 Place these feelings (achievement values) in order of importance.

3 Explore your "to-do" list and identify what actions will lead to these feelings or the achievement of these goals. They are important to you.

4 Examine the qualities of people you know and respect. What are the qualities they have as a person that make you respect them? What are the qualities that you possess that you treasure the most? What are the qualities you want to possess that you don't yet personify to your satisfaction? Write them down.

5 With the list of qualities (Personal Code Values), examine which are the most important ones to you and place them in order.

6 Look at your to-do list and make sure these tasks are in line with these qualities.

Prioritising Your Activities

> "*Most things which are urgent are not important, and most things which are important are not urgent.*"
>
> DWIGHT D. EISENHOWER

There are a number of different ways to prioritise. Once you have checked in with your values and identified your goals, you will be in a better position to know what is important to you.

A problem many people have is that there is a difference between their priorities and their realities. There are activities that they regard as the most important to them and yet they don't pay enough attention to them. For most, spending time with their family and friends is a priority yet they place other less important activities above it. They spend more time doing housework or extra hours working.

The **Eisenhower Matrix** is one of the most popular tools in time management and, in my opinion, one of the most useful. Its use should not be restricted to business life but should be expanded to fit your personal life. Conor Holmes got great use from the matrix and used it successfully to keep track of his everyday activities. Steven Covey, in his book, 7 *Habits of Highly Effective People*, describes the matrix quite coherently. Here I will give my own perspective on it.

You start by considering two concepts: What is important? What is urgent? **Important** refers to something which you deem as being something you need to do, something very valuable. **Urgent** means something that has to be done within a certain timeframe with a deadline in mind.

The Eisenhower Matrix has four quadrants. From the top left going clockwise, the first quadrant is known as IMPORTANT and URGENT. This is often for crisis management tasks and also for activities that are pressing timewise and which are also deemed to be important. These items must be dealt with immediately.

The next quadrant is for the tasks that benefit you in the long term. Being IMPORTANT and yet NOT URGENT, they are more likely to reflect your values, as they are not essential to do immediately because of time constraints. However, their importance is of a higher value, as they are more than likely activities that will have a positive impact on your future work. By doing them, you will naturally improve how you run your business and life. The idea is to reduce the other quadrants by increasing this quadrant.

The third quadrant is for the tasks that are non essentials (NOT IMPORTANT) and are not necessary to get done immediately (NOT URGENT). In a perfect world, most of them would be done but the key is to focus on getting things done in the other quadrants first and only get to the activities in this quadrant if you have time. Or simply drop them.

Quadrant four is for the tasks that are more distractions than anything else. These are things that should be done immediately (URGENT) but are not vital or essential that you do them (NOT IMPORTANT). The best thing to do is to delegate these tasks.

The more you can think ahead and get the tasks in quadrant two done (IMPORTANT and NOT URGENT) the less likely you are to have the crisis of quadrant one (IMPORTANT and URGENT). Furthermore, tasks in quadrant three (NOT IMPORTANT and NOT URGENT) should be deleted or deferred or delegated. and tasks in quadrant four (not IMPORTANT but URGENT) should be delegated to somebody else.

Exercise
Eisenhower Matrix

Create a grid like the one below and fit in the activities on your to-do list, placing each one into the corresponding box.

1 IMPORTANT & URGENT	2 IMPORTANT & NON-URGENT
4 NON-IMPORTANT & URGENT	3 NON-IMPORTANT & NON-URGENT

When you put the items from your "to-do" list into the four categories, you will find yourself getting clearer in identifying which tasks you need to do. Of course staying on top of things is imperative. This matrix is something that is useful to use when you are deciding on what to do with incoming tasks as well.

How to Turn Your Priorities into Realities

In working with your priorities, it is vital to be able to turn them into your realities. From the last section, you will have become much more aware of how you have been spending your time. From this section, you have been clarifying what is most important for you.

As discussed earlier, there is often a gap between people's perception of what is important and what they actually spend their time on. In my experience, when people realise the differences between the two they are often surprised, if not shocked. Sometimes they just sigh and shrug, which seems to imply that they think it is outside of their control.

The funny thing is, when I argue that these things are not their priorities because they haven't been giving them the time they deserve, they are quick to rebuke me. They defend their outline of what is most important to them and find every excuse in the world to defend their decisions. They say things like "I have to work"; "I am doing it for them"; "They understand"; "I can see my parents anytime"; "My friends will have a good time anyway, they don't need me."

These excuses are defence mechanisms we have developed. They serve us by protecting our own contradictions, where we say one thing and do another. The problem is, these excuses are often attempts to justify things that simply aren't useful for us. We end up spending time arguing that we are out of control of our fate and that we are doing our best when we are not.

The real key here is to begin the process of realising our priorities. This means taking each priority we say we have and making it a reality. It involves asking important questions.

Exercise

Priorities into Realities

- What actions do you need to take in order to be making your priority your reality?

- What things do you need to do on a regular basis to ensure that you prioritise in reality what you call a priority in your head?

Priorities List

- Based upon your decisions in the Eisenhower Matrix, make a decision about what things you have to do this week and have completed this week.

- Keep this list constant and do not add to it. If you think of something else, wait until you have completed everything else first.

- If you are asked to do something else but it is not as important as what you have on the list, make sure you say "No".

Once you have figured out the most important tasks, saying No is a skill that will keep you on the straight and narrow. In many ways, prioritising is a process of saying Yes to certain activities and No to others. Let's explore why, how and when we do this.

15

The Power of "No"

*"The art of being wise is the art of knowing
what to overlook."*

WILLIAM JAMES

The Power of No is one of the most important keys to a successful life management system. The word "NO" can allow you to free up a massive amount of time. Our modern-day life makes so many demands on our time that we need to be very careful as to what we say yes and no to.

KEY POINT

**Whenever we say yes to something we are
saying no to everything else.**

So, when we say Yes to extra work, we are saying No to all of the things we aren't going to be doing at that time, including maybe spending time with our family or exercising or having quality time for ourselves. The trick is to learn **why we say No, when to say No** and **how to say No**. Firstly, however, why do we say Yes?

Why We Say Yes

There are a number of different reasons why we tend to say Yes to so many things. Often we say Yes far too often and we end up taking on far too much. Some people do so because saying Yes gives them another activity for them to get wrapped up and escape in. Others do so because they have learned to say Yes habitually to whatever they have been asked to do and they hate to let other people down. There are some people who continue to say Yes to new projects in an attempt to enjoy constant stimulation. Some others do so out of a fear of missing out if they say No. Lastly, there are many out there who believe that they are superhuman and can fit everything in and like the challenge of it all.

Reason 1: Need to Escape

People often take on too much in order to escape. When they are working they don't have to face up to themselves or parts of their life that they are not happy with. They have control over their work so they use this as an opportunity to immerse themselves within what they do so as not to have to deal with the rest of their life.

It becomes convenient to be doing something productive as a means of escaping something which may not be very productive, such as ruminating over why you are single or feeling bad about a toxic relationship which you can't seem to get out of.

So, this can be something useful and good to do in certain circumstances. For example, if you have just broken up with somebody, then throwing yourself into your work for a while is not a bad option at all, especially when you compare it to the other tempting options, such as spending the next few months inebriated with drink, feeling sorry for yourself, searching for someone to replace the one that you have lost while you regale everyone with your sob story! Indeed, work is a healthy and useful option for this period of transition.

The difficulty comes when the "escape" becomes a permanent avoidance of the issues of your life, which will still be there, lurking in the background like a tired stalker, waiting to jump out of the shadows of the world and bring you back to reality with a thump.

Saying Yes to everything ensures that we are never at a loss for things in which to absorb ourselves, even when the most important things we must deal with are waiting for us. So, to avoid taking on too much in order to escape, it is useful to learn how to use work in an even more productive way and say No to those activities that do not serve our best interests.

Reason 2: Can't say No

Then there are those who seem to have the inability to say No. The strange thing is, when you tell them to say "No", they say, "No, I can't" to you. Then you point out that they have just said No and they say, "No I didn't". You try to argue but they refuse to believe it. "No. I did not say No".

Often, if you aren't aware that you have the ability to say No, it is because, in most areas of your life, it is like a bad word. When someone asks you to do something, you *must* do it. They need your help and no one else will help. And it is possible to do. Saying No would lead to catasrophe. They might think you are unable to do anything and they would never ask you again. If you said No to a customer, they would leave you, never to return again. If you said No to your partner, they might hate you. If you said No to your children, you would be a bad parent . . . and so on.

We develop these crazy associations with the word No. We feel almost as if by saying No we are rejecting others in our lives. And we don't want to reject anyone in our life. We would feel too guilty if we said No. Guilt is a huge factor for many people. Since we can't be all things to all people, it is imperative that we accept that fully and completely and make sure we become happy with doing our best.

In visiting and working in cultures such as India and Japan, I discovered that they really dislike refusing requests. Many times I asked for something and they agreed and said Yes to it, but it never happened. The politeness of their cultures ensured that they would save face, which was more important than follow-through. Of course, this isn't the same for everyone in these cultures, but occurs in certain contexts which are noticeably different to standard western business decorum. Saying Yes is often an effort to avoid offending people in power.

Reason 3: Need for Constant Stimulation

We live in a world suffering from attention defecit disorder. With instant information about anything available at our fingertips and continuous movies and television available for us to watch, we have developed a need to stimulate ourselves as much as possible. The world is whizzing by and we are expected to keep up with it. The best way to keep up with it is by taking on all that we can and staying afloat by the waves of experience that threaten to overwhelm us.

Boredom is now something which people can experience more quickly and more intensely than ever before. Because we are now using external devices more than our own brains, we look to the outside to provide us with a never-ending stream of entertainment. We also check our email a hundred times an hour because we want to be productive, stimulated and active. We want to be on top of things.

The need for constant stimulation means that we are faced with doing far more than we can handle because we want our brains continuously occupied so that we aren't wasting time. Sadly, by running ourselves into the ground, we end up wasting far more time in our busyness than we would do if we actually took a step back from things.

Reason 4: Fear of Missing Out on Things

Many people say Yes because they fear that if they say No then they might miss out on something important.

The world is alive with millions of websites and books and there is so much going on in our lives that we feel a constant need to try to keep up with it all.

We have so many choices in what we can do that we don't want to miss out on anything and we don't want our children to miss out on anything either. So we say Yes to the expensive Christmas presents and Yes to the dozens of after-school activities, not pausing for a second to evaluate if there is a better way of spending time.

There is a fear many people have that they will regret what they didn't do, so they try to do everything and try to be involved in everything to compensate. However, by doing so, they miss what matters most and they forget that they are saying No to everything else when they say Yes to yet another activity or task. Nobody likes to feel out of the loop and the failure to participate could result in such a consequence.

Reason 5: Superhuman Delusions

To a degree, most of us have superhuman delusions. Indeed, most of the people I work with have superhuman beliefs about what they could accomplish. Take some participants in the *Not Enough Hours* programmes, for example. Conor pushed himself way over the limit in his ambitions of what he could take on. Siobhan's need for control meant she took on far more than was healthy for her. Marina's search for perfection had her attempting to create the perfect life for everyone concerned while maintaining perfect health simultaneously.

Michael's desire to help ensured that he took on more positions and more roles in the community than any typical person would even consider. Olivia's warped sense of time resulted in her mythical belief that she could make a one-hour journey in 15 minutes. Margaret took on more appointments than anyone else while managing and running the entire business and bringing up a young family and skipping tea breaks and lunchtime, running her health into the ground.

Ann did so much in managing to survive in a world where traditional ways of thinking about time failed her, by somehow fighting against the odds to struggle with the indestructible enemy known as time. Dara and Ray attempted to fit in perfectly with the twins' schedule in order to be the best parents they could possibly be.

These, and many of the other people I have worked with had, to some extent, a delusion that they could manage things or that they had to work in ways that demanded far too much from them. Part of my job was getting them to accept what they could do and what was not healthy for them to try to do, so that they could make the decisions that made the greatest difference to them. When we say Yes it is because we believe we are capable of doing everything that is being asked of us, yet we are really revealing a flawed way of thinking.

What many of us do is identify some time in the past where we managed to do far more than we thought we could handle; or we remember a time where we managed to fit in a lot more activities before we left the house and still made it on time. Then, we reason to ourselves that we are still okay and haven't broken down yet, therefore we are capable of it.

We want others to see our best side and we want people to think of us as being very competent and skilled. A No seems almost like an admission of incompetence. Lastly, this becomes the norm that we expect of ourselves. We expect ourselves to be capable of everything and that it will not affect us negatively and we are sometimes shocked when it does. All our Yeses are breaking us down.

So, now that we understand the different reasons why we say Yes, we must understand the importance of learning to say No. We don't have to say No to everything and all the time. We simply have to remember that Yes and No go hand-in-hand and by saying No to one thing we are saying Yes to something else and vice versa. That will allow us to make this habit easier to follow through.

Why Say No?

When you have a good understanding about what your priorities are, you will be in a position where you will need to say No to certain activities. What this means is, you will have to stand by and support your priorities once you have decided on them.

Of course, there will be many challenges which attempt to take your attention away or convince you to engage in other tasks in place of what you have prioritised. It is crucial for you to be able to say No in those circumstances.

Just like there are some reasons why we say Yes to more tasks, there are a number of reasons why we need to say No more often. We need to realise that No is Yes and Yes is No in different contexts; that saying No can help you avoid stress and burnout; that saying No improves your self-esteem and ensures that you don't miss out on experiences in your life that really matter. Finally, saying No allows you to get full control over your life because you are actively choosing what kind of life you want to lead.

No is Yes and Yes is No

To me, one of the most important of all time management concepts is that No is Yes and Yes is No. By that I mean that every Yes you say is a No to everything else you have to do in your life. By saying Yes, you need to make sure that you are fully happy that this activity is the very best use of your time right then and there.

When you say No to something, you are saying Yes to you being able to choose from all of the other things you could be doing and you get to decide what is the most important activity right then and there.

"No" is the key word which can lead you to the path of successful prioritising. It ensures that you are focused on what truly matters.

Destroy Stress and Burnout

Every time you say Yes to another activity, you are piling more and more things to do on top of everything else on your schedule. The more you do this, the more stress and anxiety you are inflicting upon yourself. GPs report that stress has become one of the biggest problems at the root cause of many medical problems every day. The problem of burnout is widespread these days and, as we have learned earlier, in Japan, there are even statistics on *Karoshi*, which refers to people dying from burnout and working too much.

Saying No is truly a way of saying Yes to your own health. Every time you refuse something which is a task too much, you are ensuring that you have time to do the things which are good for you. Of course, it is a good idea to say Yes to regular trips to the gym, healthy food; a good night's sleep and even a nice massage or spa trip from time to time. Saying No to an obsessive amount of work can actually make you more productive and efficient as well.

Overwork can easily lead to stress and burnout, which can lead to sick days, which often results in far more work to do when you return to work. So, saying No is actually something which can help you save yourself from stress and burnout as well as ensuring you can work at your best when you most need to.

Build Self-Esteem

Saying No can have a terrific impact upon your self-esteem. Every time you say No to another person's request because there is something else that you prioritise, you are affirming your own ability to follow your own counsel.

It can be easy to let others pressure us into doing more than we should. When you learn to say No, it lets you stand up to others so that they won't succeed in walking all over you and manipulating you into doing whatever they want. Saying No is a declaration of personal freedom which suggests that, although you will do your best to help, you will only do so in a way that is conducive to your personal wellbeing and in a way that is in alignment with your personal goals.

It is also good for your reputation. If you are the kind of person who can say No, it means that you value your time and therefore your time must be valuable. The way you treat yourself will often lead others to treat you in the same way.

Be There for the Important Experiences

While we can fear that saying No can rob us of potential experiences, we must remember that saying Yes can do the very same thing. When we say No to something, we give ourselves the opportunity to say Yes to other things that are more important. For example, saying No to that extra workshop can allow us to see our son's football final or our daughter's play.

It allows us to experience the things that matter the most. We get to ensure that we are spending the moments of our lives in the situations that are most important to us. When we are dying on our deathbeds, it is the memories we have to cherish with our families that we will most remember with fond nostalgia. By saying No to other unnecessary events, we allow ourselves to take the time to experience the wonderful moments.

Control Your Life

Many people find themselves stuck in a rut, overwhelmed by a massive number of things to do, running around in circles trying to catch up. Saying No is such an important step in taking charge and control of your life. When you refuse to do something, you are choosing how you spend your moments. That sense of choice is a feeling of control that helps you feel better about your life.

When you say No you are being mindful about how you are spending your time. Of course, there are times when it is hard to say No but if you always remember that you are doing it for the right reasons, then you will find yourself well capable of doing it.

When to Say No?

Once you have set your priorities and organised your schedule, it should be easy to know when to say No. Whenever someone asks you to do something that you haven't already scheduled in, you need to examine what they are asking you to do and see which is more important overall – what they are asking you or what you have already planned.

The answer to this question should determine whether or not you say Yes or No to them. Every decision you make about incoming requests for your attention or actions should be evaluated according to whether it is urgent and important, as you learned in the Eisenhower Matrix. Once you have done this, the next key is to decide, if it is not important, whether you should delegate it or just refuse to take it on.

So when someone asks you to do something, you must weigh it up against what you have already scheduled for that time and make a decision based upon that comparison. It is really important that, before you decide when to say No, you have a clear understanding of your priorities. It is also essential that you have decided to make your priorities actionable and make them realities so that it is not just what you "say" that is important, but more so what you do.

In fact, it would probably be a better way of thinking about it if you considered when to say Yes. Deciding when to say Yes should be something you become much more mindful of and therefore which you treat with more discrimination. You should only say Yes when you are absolutely convinced that spending time in the activity is a priority and will reward you sufficiently.

By looking at what you have prioritised and what is being asked of you, you will soon find it very easy to know when you need to say Yes and when to say No. Once you have decided to say No, however, the next issue will be *how* you do that. It will be important for you to be able to do so without damaging the relationship with the other person. So, let us examine the different ways you say No most usefully.

How to say No?

For some people, saying No is something really challenging. To refuse someone a request is so difficult. Once you get to the point where you realise how vital it is to learn how to say No, the next step is for you to actually practise saying No to people. When you first start saying

No you will find yourself feeling a little guilty or concerned at first. That's simply a result of doing something different to what you have done before. It's important to get used to this feeling. Once you do, you will find it far easier to say No. Soon, it will turn into a feeling of freedom as you start to choose your own way more.

To get good at it, start small on simple requests that don't matter and get experience with those. There are, of course, a number of ways to say No which minimise the chances of it making either you or the other person feel bad. Keep remembering in your mind, *you are always saying No*, it is a question of what you are saying No to.

So let's look at some of the most useful ways to say No. Firstly, the key is that whenever you say No, always do it with empathy. Acknowledge the importance of what the other person wants done and express your sympathy, empathy or apologies if you cannot help them, before you launch into one of the effective ways of saying No. There are six techniques for saying No that you might find useful:

- Reasonable No
- Alternative No
- Deferred No
- Soft No
- Broad No
- Obvious No

Reasonable No

A Reasonable No is simply a No with a reason as to why not. It explains the situation clearly to the other person and let's them know why you are saying No. It is a good idea to really emphasise how important this other activity is to you.

Example:

> *"Will you please fit this extra project in on Saturday?"*

> *"I can't fit in that extra project because I promised the kids I'd spend the day with them. It's the first day in a while I get to do so and I really can't wait to see how they are getting on with all the new things they have been learning in school."*

Alternative No

You can say No but immediately suggest an alternative. Most Nos work well when you offer alternatives. It shows that you are being helpful and trying to make sure they get the result they are looking for. It's just that you already have something as a priority lined up for yourself. You could suggest that they contact someone else who might be able to help.

Example:

> *"Can you mind the kids on Friday evening?"*

> *"Unfortunately, No, but have you tried checking in with Mark? He might be able to help you."*

Deferred No

You can also give them a deferred No. This is not necessarily saying No but saying "When?" It is stating that you will help; it's just a matter of time.

Example:

> *"Can you help me with this?"*
>
> *"When? I can't help you now but how about a time that works for both of us?"*

Soft No

You can say No without actually using the word "No". By telling them what else you have on – and sometimes by pre-empting their request and mentioning something you have at that time – you can avoid them asking or pushing you to do something.

Example:

> *"I have lots to do and I'm looking for someone to help me with it."*
>
> *"My goodness, that is a lot to do. I have a lot to do myself as well this weekend. I think I'll be more tired at the end of the weekend than I am at the end of the week!"*

Broad No

You can say a broad No but then suggest a potential alternative. This is when you say No to far more than what they are asking for and then suggesting an option which is different to what they have asked for.

Example:

> *"I want an appointment with you today please."*
>
> *"Unfortunately, I have no space available at all this week really, but, hang on – maybe tomorrow I can*

just about fit you in if you can make it between 12.00 and 12.30."

Obvious No

You can say an obvious No which presupposes that it is impossible to accommodate their request but that you will do your best at another time or under different circumstances. You can use words like "obviously" or "clearly".

Example:

"Can you pick something up in the shops for me today?"

"Obviously, as you can see, I have far too much to do today to have time to do that but I might be able to get it tomorrow or the day after if I get time."

Evaluate how much time you are spending doing things for others and how much time you are spending on yourself. Decide to spend more time on yourself. Time for yourself is necessity time, *not* luxury time. Remember, by saying No, you are never letting other people down, instead you are making a call on what is most important. Set yourself time deadlines to go and spend quality time that matters.

Make sure that you make time for your meals, exercise and time out for yourself and do not allow other peoples' demands to encroach on this time. The way in which you say No can help you to keep people on-side, even when you reject their request or refuse them. The

key is to demonstrate empathy and make it clear that you
do care but you have other things that you have already
prioritised. Reasonable people will understand and those
who don't aren't being very reasonable.

Saying No and prioritising what is most important to
you is essential. Once you have done this, however, there
are still a couple of steps left to take on your journey
towards using your time brilliantly. The next step is to
take full control over how you organise your life.

ORGANISE

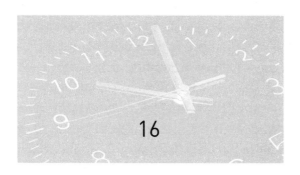

16

The Art of Organising

"The secret of all victory lies in the organisation of the non-obvious."

MARCUS AURELIUS

Do you find yourself spending much of your time trying to locate something that you stored away somewhere safe before? Have you missed your bus, train, plane or an important meeting because you got the wrong time? Ever find yourself overwhelmed with so many tasks that you don't know where to begin? If so, your main issue is a lack of organisation.

In this section I want to look at what it means to organise your life and your time and reveal what I have found to be the most useful tips and skills to do so. These tips and skills are not just what I use myself but those I have used with thousands of people to help them in their lives.

Given the excessive amount of information we have to deal with these days in all its different forms, we need to organise ourselves better than ever before. In order to do so, we must achieve a number of outcomes. We need to find a way of capturing information intelligently. We need to create an effective and efficient system of organising information as it comes at us. We need to develop a disciplined habit of using this system and placing things where they belong. We need to learn to schedule and plan productively so that we understand what is in store for us.

When I first started working on the RTÉ show, I had already arranged my schedule to fit in with the rest of my life. I had to balance the TV work with my other work as a trainer, therapist and consultant. I also arranged to have some time off during some of the weekends I wasn't working and made sure that I was able to switch off completely from everything right the way through the whole experience.

Now, the fact that I had the time organised made things a lot easier for me. In my room is my wall planner, which highlights exactly where I need to be at any given moment in time and what I am doing. This wall planner and my diary allow me to keep track of everything constantly. I went continuously from meeting to meeting and had to keep track of the different ideas, issues and problems that arose. If I hadn't been organised, I would never have been able to help, much less understand what was going on.

Flying as often as I do requires an extensive amount of booking of flights and hotels, as well as arrangements for the destination in question. Having been on 93 flights in 2007, the vast majority of which I arranged myself, I have to be very organised. In order to get everything I need to do successfully completed, it is critical that I have a system that lets me organise my life in an easy and simple way.

I have a very different way of organising myself than most people I know. I have tried many different organisational techniques and strategies and therefore have found an enormous variety of ideas that appeal to different types of people. What works for me may not always appear exceptionally organised on the outside, but it fits me perfectly.

With all the different demands I take on board, I see it as organised chaos. A million demands being thrown at you is a huge challenge to attempt to manage or organise, but there is a way to do it. Of course, having children is another real case of organised chaos. You can't predict exactly what is going to happen on a day-to-day basis when children enter the equation. All you can do is learn to have an outline of a plan and do your best to respond to whatever comes up as it comes up.

The principle of organising chaos is that there is no such thing as having everything perfectly organised. Chaos will always exist. Unforeseen events will always occur. Our treasured Murphy's Law may crop up. But the key is that, regardless of what happens, we can develop a system whereby we deal with whatever comes up in the most effective way.

Of course, some people are comfortable with planning while others find plans more challenging. "Planners" tend to be more proactive, organised, prepared and structured. They are more likely to remember your birthday, for example. They can also spend a large amount of time planning for events, but sometimes too much time.

"Responders" are more spontaneous, flexible, open and adventurous. They like deadlines and are more comfortable with last-minute actions. They hate planning and work much better by the seat of their pants.

The key is that, regardless of whether or not you are a "planner" or a "responder", you can find your own preferred way of scheduling and organising yourself. Your schedules can be as flexible as you need them to be, but it is essential that you have some way of keeping track of your activities.

Now, when I talk about keeping track, I am not talking about keeping track inside your head. I am talking about having some sort of system on the outside that allows you to do so. What fascinates me most about the people I have worked with is that few of them use calendars, diaries or wall planners regularly and consistently. In fact, many of them hold their demanding schedules inside their heads. To me, this notion is ridiculous. It's crazy to consider the idea that we can accurately and easily hold all of our tasks for the day in our mind. Since I began working, I always spent time scheduling on paper what I had to do. Even when you have an aversion to planning, it's still necessary to engage in some kind of scheduling for the future. Often people will make excuses that they don't have enough time to plan. The truth is, however, when you do plan, you will save far more time as a result.

Whether using "to do" lists, a Filofax or a diary, I have always planned and dated everything I was doing or had to do. In the modern world, we have far too many activities to keep track of at any given moment in time. Thus, the need for **external memory** is necessary. We have already covered the need for "to do" lists in the previous section but here I want to examine other ways of scheduling.

There are two different types of projects we usually take on. The first is regarded as a **continuous project** whereas the second is an **organisational project**. The continuous project might be something like keeping your accounts in order while the organisational project usually involves breaking something into smaller tasks in order to tackle it bit by bit to meet a certain deadline. Either way, each project involves certain tasks which we have to do and which we need to schedule into our life.

The first step is to adopt a system that you can use to deal with whatever tasks and activities come your way. This system – **the 4D System** – is designed to maximise how effectively and efficiently you work.

The 4D System: Do, Defer, Delegate and Delete

Since we can't do everything ourselves, we need to ensure that we **do** what we can do, **defer** what we can't do now but can do later, **delegate** what we can get someone else to do and **delete** what we can't do and what isn't necessary to do.

This system is a powerful way of ensuring that we make steady, significant progress with the tasks that are given to us. It relies upon our ability to let go of the need to do everything ourselves. In order to make this system work, we first need to feel comfortable with not doing certain things, with holding off on things that are not urgent and, finally, with giving some of our tasks to someone else. For many people, these three tasks are challenging to fulfil. Many of us have become control freaks in this society, simply because we have so much more power to control things than ever before.

The beauty of this system lies in its simplicity. Everything that demands your time is either something you need to do right away, something you can do later, something you can ask someone else to do or something you really don't need to do.

By dividing all work you have into these categories, you can effectively ensure that you are working to the priorities you have decided upon. When you are clear what are the most important elements for you to do, you can ensure that you are doing them. This works quite nicely with the Eisenhower Matrix, discussed in Chapter 14.

The important and urgent tasks need to be done. Meanwhile, the important and non-urgent tasks can be deferred until the next day. The non-important and urgent tasks are probably best delegated whereas the non-important and non-urgent tasks are best deleted.

You really need to make sure that, once you start using this system, it becomes a habit for you. When you do that, you will find yourself effectively starting to free up more time. Your decisions on what you deem to be your top priorities will influence how you deal with whatever information you receive. The key, therefore, is to make well-informed and smart decisions on which of the 4Ds to use with each piece of information you receive.

This is not just a work strategy. This is a life strategy. Whenever your child asks you to bring them to the swimming pool, you can either do it, get someone else to drop them there, promise to bring them later or not do it at all. This will depend on a number of factors, including how important this activity might be for your family members and not just for yourself. The key is to understand that your choices on how you fulfil your family responsibilities will affect the relationships you have with them.

What is important is that you make the best decisions at that time. The way you will know if they are the best decisions will be your investigation into your goals, values and priorities.

When you are deciding whether or not to do something, you should examine which category it fits into. Just because you think you should do something because it's a priority doesn't mean that you should do it straight away. You need to remember that timing can be crucial with certain actions.

At certain times the information you receive may not require you to do anything. Instead, it simply requires you to put it away somewhere in case you might need to use it as a reference in the future. So, have somewhere to put this material. With the tasks you have to do, use this 4Ds system.

To explain this system, let's look at an example of someone with a number of tasks to do. Lisa is a stylist. She is in the middle of writing a book about fashion. At the same time, she has been asked to write an article for a national newspaper. Her brother wants her to pick him up from town and she also plans to go to a wedding fair.

Do It:

If you can immediately do the action and it is important and valuable to do, then you can do it then and there. Also, if there is a part of it that you can do immediately that will diminish the task you have to do, then do that then and there and defer the rest of the task. As the newspaper article is an important and potentially valuable way of marketing her business, Lisa decides to write the article first thing.

Defer It:

If you can't do the task then and there, then do one thing: schedule in when specifically you can do it. Define a date and a time and give yourself enough time to do it. Although writing the book is important for Lisa, she knows that she doesn't need to do it urgently and so she defers the book writing until later in the day.

Delete It:

Does this really need to be done? If not, then simply don't do it. Delete it from your "to-do" list. Say No. Lisa likes wedding fairs and seeing all the various offers on store but she is not engaged and going to the fair is not urgent or important, so she decides not to go.

Delegate It:

If someone else can do it for you and save time, ask them to do it. Make sure when you do so that you are aware that it is important *how* you delegate. Instead of picking her brother up herself, Lisa calls her friend who is in town and lives nearby and asks her to pick him up instead. This works out perfectly.

The Importance of Delegation

You must master the art of delegation if you wish to save time. Whether you are doing so in your business or with your family responsibilities, the importance of getting someone else's help to do it cannot be underestimated.

Many people refuse to delegate because they believe that nobody will be able to do a job as well as they will. They feel like the work will suffer and they are anxious when someone else takes over. What this leads to is more anxiety and pressure, which causes them to feel guilty and obliged to take back control of everything again.

Delegation requires trust. This means you need to be able to hand over tasks to others and trust that they will be done and done well. You may need to stick closely to the person and initially to do the task with them in order to develop that trust, but you must arrange it so that you can then happily let go of the responsibility.

I worked with a couple where the wife tended to take on the responsibility for the vast majority of the housework. The husband was prepared to chip in and help but he was unable to, because she wouldn't allow him to do anything much as she believed that he

227

"wouldn't do it right". I encouraged her to become open to the fact that: a) things didn't need to be done "right" her way all the time; and b) he could get most jobs done pretty well and it was important to allow him to do so.

It's essential to delegate as soon as possible. The more time you waste thinking about it, the less effective the solution will be. It's a great idea to create some extra buffer time when you do delegate something. This is in the event that something needs changing when you check it or in case the person delivers the action past the original deadline.

If you can give people a specific deadline for the end of the task; and also split up the task into smaller chunks and give them deadlines along the way for each "chunk", against which they can measure their productiveness; and remind them before the final deadline; that will help ensure that your delegation proves successful. Following up immediately and not tolerating excuses is useful as well.

Delegating a project or a task also requires that you become effective at selecting the right person in the right area. Sometimes delegating is simply about asking someone to do something for you. Sometimes, however, it is a far bigger decision. Take Margaret, for example, the hair salon owner whom I worked with on the *Not Enough Hours* show.

Margaret learned from the work we did together that she needed an assistant manager in the office. She needed someone to look after things so she could take a step back in order to grow the business, as well as look after herself and spend better quality time with her children. So

Margaret hired an assistant manager to help her to do just that. Of course, there was a financial cost involved in hiring someone new; however, the benefit accrued by the appointment freed up her precious time to really grow the business.

Whether it's a big decision like this or a spur of the moment decision, the key is to make sure that you are fully prepared to allow other people to help and to ask them for help so that you can become more efficient and effective.

The guilt factor is something else to look at and overcome. Often, when we ask others to do something, we feel guilty for doing so. Maybe you feel guilty about asking your mother to mind the kids after school or for leaving your children with someone else when you feel you should be minding them yourself. The key to overcoming guilt around delegation is to figure out if delegating is your best option. If you think through all the options and it is, then it means that you are making the best decision you possibly can and doing the very best you possibly can. This knowledge can allow you successfully to rid yourself of much of the guilt.

When asking someone to do something, there are a number of things you can do to maximise their chances of saying Yes. People will respond more positively to requests with a good attitude attached, those that are well timed, those from which they will also benefit and those which seem easy and straightforward. Of course, if the person works for you, then you don't need to convince them to help you. You can simply be straightforward with them.

How to Delegate

1 Find out if the person is able to do it or already has too much on their workload. Make sure you approach them when they are in a non-stressed state.

2 Examine whether or not there is anything you can help them with so that you can offer your services as a reciprocal response to them helping you. In the event that they work for you, there is no need to do this, assuming that what you are asking lies within their job description.

3 Ensure that you use a certain and confident tone of voice when asking them. Be very clear in terms of what you want and suggest how it may be possible to do.

4 Be specific about how you want it done if the method itself is important. Make sure they can explain it back to you.

5 Look to delegate to people who are in the specific location of the task or have a skill related to the task if possible.

6 "Sell it" to them if necessary. Explain the benefits that will occur as a result of doing it and why you can't do it yourself.

Building a Better Brain

One of the things that helps greatly in the quest for becoming more organised is developing a better brain. By this I mean improving your memory, focus, concentration and absorption skills.

Building a Better Memory

Firstly, let's talk about improving your memory. Remembering things can save you a lot of time. It means you no longer have to go searching for information or take extra steps to ensure that you have everything you need. Instead, you have what information you need when you need it. One powerful tool you can use to maximise your memory is "Mind Maps".

Mind Maps®

Mind Maps are the brainchild of Tony Buzan. They are graphical maps that we create to keep track of ideas. They work more effectively for some people because they allow the person to have a more established visual representation of the concepts that they wish to remember.

Mind Maps are a terrific way of remembering and capturing ideas and tasks in a way that suits the brain. You can create a Mind Map by writing the central concept in the middle and then by creating curved, coloured branches which connect to different aspects of this concept, and then further branches which connect to aspects of each of these smaller concepts (see below). Since the brain works best by stimulation and association, the coloured curved branches are most likely to be remembered.

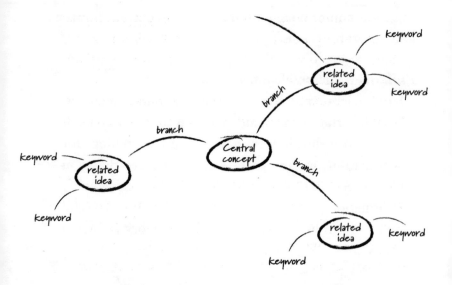

When you create a visual Mind Map of the ideas or tasks to remember, you will find it easier to remember them and you will be able to visualise the Mind Map in a quick way so that you can recall what you need to more easily. If you decide to use a Mind Map to schedule activities, the trick is to ensure that you have some way of knowing which task comes first and that each item is dated.

When I worked with artist Ann Mulrooney, I taught her Mind Maps as I knew her artistic brilliance would make it far easier for her to remember by using her visual imagination. Her ability to visualise was so good it was scary. In order to test herself after creating her first Mind Map, she closed her eyes and recalled everything in it; her visual memory of it was close to flawless. Her accuracy even surprised me.

For some people, linear lists might, in some circumstances, be effective, but others will find Mind Maps profoundly useful. They can allow you to capture schedules, ideas and concepts more easily.

Information on Mind Maps included by kind permission of Tony Buzan; www.buzanworld.com

Story Image Streaming

Story image streaming is a technique which involves making up a ridiculous story and inserting weird images into the story to create associations with the things you want to remember. The weirder the story, the better, as the brain works very well with imagination and strangeness. The odder something is, the more likely it is to stand out and be remembered. Once you have made up your story, as you go through each image in the story, it will remind you of what you want to remember.

Our brain has a natural pattern which makes it easy to follow and remember stories. The many connections and associations and the fact that one event leads to another ensure that we can easily remember the basic events of stories more quickly than unconnected information or facts.

For example, suppose you need to remember to do the laundry, wash the dishes, buy a new kettle, pick up your son from football training and pay for the flights for your holiday to Spain, you could create a story like this:

You walk into your kitchen for a cup of tea holding the milk but the kettle explodes and you

*drop the milk all over your nice top. You immediately
put it into the wash and get a glass of water instead but
there are no clean glasses, so you do the washing up.
Then a football smashes through the window and you
angrily give out to the boys who kicked it. When you
go outside it is snowing and you run back to your
house where you make a wish that you lived in a
warmer climate like Spain.*

When Ann used story image streaming, it made a
huge difference to her as it helped her create
something on which to tag information. Because she
could use her imagination brilliantly, she was able to
incorporate the information she wanted to
remember into the story so it came to her easily. It
really is a terrific way of building a much better
memory.

Building a More Focused Mind

Focus comes from dealing successfully with
distractions, which can take your attention away from
what you should be doing. There are some great tips
on dealing with distractions and interruptions in
Section 2. Often we get distracted because we are
carrying around important and unimportant thoughts
about lots of different things at once. We also can
detract from how effective we are when we multi-task
in the wrong situations. Finally, we lose focus as a
result of tiredness and lethargy. Learning to switch off,
to multi-task effectively and to improve our energy
levels are three ways to keep our minds focused and
sharp.

Switching Off

Since we live in a world of blurred boundaries, it is becoming harder and harder to **switch off** from work. I noticed a few years ago that the only time I felt I could completely relax was when I was on a plane. Nobody could call me or email me. For that flight, at least, I was free. I soon realised that this was a ridiculous situation. I needed to overcome my addiction to work in all areas of my life.

The Blackberry, iPhone, laptop and mobile phone are all devices which allow us to check our email and keep in touch with people wherever we are. More and more people are contacting us after hours and at weekends and we are expected to drop everything and respond in the moment.

Stories of people bringing their phones into spas, laptops onto the beach and Blackberries into the bathroom are no longer exaggerated tales of what we might do in extreme circumstances. They are fast becoming "normality".

One of the most essential parts of curing an addiction to work, as well as building better focus, is through learning how to switch off. This involves creating a boundary between your work and the rest of your life. Here are some ideas on how to do that:

- Explore how you feel when you switch off. What kinds of things are going through your mind? How do you feel?

- Find some ritual you can use which signals to you that you are switching modes.

- When leaving the office, turn off all the appliances deliberately and do not take any work home with you, so that you associate work only with the office. This provides the brain with closure.

- Write out a task list for the next day each day before you leave work so that the work and thoughts about work are left on external memory.

- Turn off mobiles, pager, computers and take the phone off the hook to really switch off.

The Art of Multi-tasking

There is much confusion over **multi-tasking** in the field of psychology. Some researchers are convinced that multi-tasking is a bad idea and leads to poor performance. Other researchers suggest that it actually leads to the same success in performance and far lower stress levels. How you approach multi-tasking very much depends on the tasks.

If one of your tasks is very automatic and not very important, then it is easy to do something else while you do it. Play around with the different tasks you have to do and decide which ones go together successfully without taking away from your productivity or efficiency. The problem with multi-tasking arises when we try to do two things which both require effort or concentration at the same time. We are thus moving our attention from one to the other and this results in an endless experience of distraction.

Instead, you can avoid losing focus on either task by ensuring that one of them requires no mental effort and is something that can be done automatically. This frees up the majority of your mind to keep focused on what you are learning.

For example, ironing or washing dishes while listening to an audio book or learning a language are activities that can be paired together. Since ironing or washing dishes require minimal mental effort, you can do them on autopilot and ensure that the rest of your mind is focused on something you need concentration for.

How to Maximise your Energy

Maximising your energy levels involves doing a number of things:

Live in harmony with your body clock by following the guidelines suggested in Chapter 3. This ensures that you get enough sleep and rest, which has profound effects on your energy. There will obviously be periods of the day where clock-dependent alerting means you are at your most alert. Organise activities which require energy in these periods.

Avoid drinking coffee to artificially manufacture more of these alert periods. It is not a good idea and is not all that far removed from stacking yourself up on sugary foods, which gives you a bit of a kick that lasts for a while but soon wears off, to the detriment of your body clock.

Adjust your diet to provide yourself with a more abundant supply of long-term energy. Become a student of the foods you eat and find out which foods work best for your body.

Ensure that you partake in activities which help you to de-stress and wind down. Use a worry book to write down your worries. This will assist you in getting rid of the mental clutter that might be drawing some of your energy unnecessarily.

Exercise regularly. The more you do, the more you improve how much energy you are using therefore how much you have available in your body.

Try this technique for improving your energy flow. Touch your knees twice with your hands and then place your right hand on your nose and your left hand on your right ear. Then swap around and place your left hand on your nose and your right hand on your left ear. Keep doing this and you will find yourself using both sides of your brain, feeling more creative and having more energy.

If you need a burst of energy for a set period of time, you can use the **mental energy booster** as described below.

Exercise

Mental Energy Booster

1 This booster is a very quick and powerful way of boosting your energy for a specific period of time when you need it most.

2   Ask yourself, "How much energy do I need and for how long?"

3   Make a commitment to yourself that you will pay back in sleep any extra sleep you miss out on or any extra energy you use as a result of doing this. (Make sure you follow through on this commitment!)

4   Close your eyes and imagine a time when you felt at your most energised. Remember what you saw, heard and felt. Vividly experience it inside your mind. Imagine energy flooding through your entire body and filling you up, making you feel alive with energy.

5   Imagine yourself doing whatever you need to do, feeling fully recharged for the entire period.

6   Breathe deeply a number of times. With each breath in, imagine that you are breathing in your life force; with each breath out, imagine you are breathing out tiredness.

7   Then, open your eyes and stretch, and tense and relax your muscles and change your physiology into an energised posture. Straighten your body and stand ready for action.

The Organisation of Your Mind

For the last fifteen years, I've helped people run their brains in more effective ways. By learning from some of the top experts in the field of personal development, such as Dr Richard Bandler, I've gained some wonderful understandings about how our minds work. The final area that I want to talk about to help you build a better brain is to learn how you can organise your mind more effectively.

Since Freud came along in the late nineteenth century, we have understood the mind to be made up of a conscious and an unconscious part. The conscious mind is viewed as the part of our mind which we use to navigate our way through the world. It is where we hold our ability to focus and to think rationally, logically and reasonably.

The unconscious mind is seen as the storehouse for all our memories, wisdom and perceptions. Whereas the conscious mind seems to rest as the body goes to sleep, the unconscious never does. It is not only a storage place but it regulates our blood pressure, breathing and heart. It is where our circadian rhythm operates.

This metaphor for the brain being comprised of a conscious and an unconscious mind is a useful way of describing how we think, as it explains much of our experience in the world. Using this metaphor, we can understand that many of our habits become automated, unconscious habits after much conscious practice. Indeed, many of the new habits you will be acquiring as you implement the changes in this book will become unconscious after you practise them a few times.

Our inner worlds are where we live regardless of where we go. We spend every day of our lives inside our own heads. The key is to make sure that this "world" is a wonderful place to live. Amazingly, we have the ability to do that. Whereas in the outside world, we must rely on others helping us, we have control in our own minds. When someone tries to keep their town tidy, they can't guarantee that others will follow suit. But they can determine how clean their mind is.

There are some fantastic approaches to help you improve your own brain. I highly recommend concepts such as NLP (Neuro-Linguistic Programming), hypnosis and meditation. **NLP** is an attitude and method which helps you think more effectively, perform more effectively and communicate more effectively. **Hypnosis** allows you to enter a state of mind where you can more easily communicate with your unconscious. **Meditation** similarly allows you to enter a state of mind where you are free from as many thoughts as possible and so calm that you are training your brain to become that way more of the time.

To start off with here, let's examine how you can organise your mind more effectively and deal with the biggest time-wasting feelings that you face.

The State of Your Mind

The way you feel is created by the thoughts that you think. Our thoughts create the feelings we experience. Many of these thoughts can creep up on you and immediately trigger a negative state. The trick is to learn how you can take control over your mind and arrange it so that you no longer go straight into these negative states.

There are two elements of which you need to be aware. Firstly, your **physiology** will make it easier or harder for you to go into a particular state. For example, if you are smiling, it is easier to feel happy and harder to feel sad. The trick is to physiologically move into the posture of the state with the same expression you would have.

The second element is that you can change your state by being **aware** of how you are thinking and how those thoughts create your feelings. Once you have this awareness, simply start generating thoughts that make you feel the way you want to feel.

It's also important to eliminate feelings which erode our time. These feelings include guilt, disapproval anxiety, stress and fear.

Guilt

Often guilt is something which eats away at people when we talk about saving time. When you are organising your mind more effectively, it's important that you learn to avoid filling it up with as much guilt as you have been.

Guilt is a signal that we send to our minds which suggests that we need to take a careful look at our behaviour, as it may be out of line with our values or what we feel is the right thing to do. The feeling of guilt is designed to get us to double-check on things and to learn to do the right thing.

The way you can deal with guilt and minimise its appearance is to accept this positive intention. Instead of fighting the guilty feelings, you accept them and ask them what they are trying to make you more aware of. Once you find the answer to this, you next analyse whether or not you are doing the right thing and whether or not you should change things.

For example, suppose you are spending time studying at college and you feel guilty about the fact that your children are missing out on time with you. Rather than immediately giving in to the guilt and quitting college, or overcompensating by spoiling your children, you can find out what the intention of this guilt is. Most probably, it will be to remind you that it is essential that you keep prioritising quality time with your children. You can continue studying in college but by making up some free time for your children and ensuring you make the most of it, you can feel better about the time you are spending at college as well.

When you think things through and feel that you are doing the very best you can, this reminder will help you quash the feelings of guilt. Also, in the event that others try to make you feel guilty, you will become much more aware that this is *their* game and therefore you can refuse to participate in it.

Disapproval Anxiety

Some people find themselves struggling as a result of feeling bad because they fear disapproval. They feel bad because others criticise them or are nasty to them. They worry what other people think. Being too concerned with other people's thoughts about you might mean that you allow others to control you or that you act in ways that are not useful for you, just to satisfy others.

Building a brain independent enough to be free from the need to satisfy others will happen when you change the way you think about other people's

243

feedback. Whenever you get feedback from someone, separate the feedback about you as a person from feedback about your behaviour. Recognise that the feedback they give you about yourself is never accurate, as you are who you decide to be.

Their perception is based upon your behaviour, which is something different. When you accept this difference, you will find yourself being okay with what others think or say because they are simply remarking about your behaviour, which you can change (or you can choose not to change it if you decide that the feedback is inaccurate).

Stress

People become stressed because they think in stressful ways. They worry and think about all the problems they have and this can manifest itself physically in their bodies. There is plenty of research to suggest that stress is much more a manifestation of a lack of control over your time than it is a problem with a lack of time itself.

One technique for developing a stress-free mind involves writing down any of your worries or problems and deciding on an action plan for each of the stresses that you can do something about. If the problem is particularly daunting, then simply break the solution down into a number of different steps which are easier to implement. In the event that there is nothing you can do about a problem, the mere process of writing it down will get it out of your head and onto paper.

Taking more time to be in the present is crucial. Stress usually comes from our regrets of the past or our worries about the future. Stress typically doesn't exist in the present. So, if you bring your awareness to what you see, hear, feel, smell and taste in the moment, you will find yourself enjoying the experience of staying in the present. This simple technique is the cornerstone of a powerful movement inspired by books such as *The Power of Now* and is a very popular, basic yet effective stress reliever.

Often we do many things because we feel we *have* to do them. When you realise that you do have a choice whether or not to do them, you will instantly feel more in charge of your life.

There are lots of other ways to help yourself build a stress-free brain – grounding yourself in nature, exercising, meditating, eating better, sleeping well and changing your attitude towards life. In section 7, you'll find some more tips on freeing your time from stress.

Fear

Fear is a signal that our brains send us to warn us of something. Whereas thousands of years ago, our fears protected us from being killed by dangerous animals, nowadays most of our fears are not nearly as useful. When we are scared, we stop ourselves doing things that we know would make our lives better. We waste a lot of time being scared of rejection, failure or embarrassment.

Overcoming our fears is about identifying what scares us and accepting that if we actually were to experience what we fear, it would probably not make much of a difference to our lives. It is about learning to change the meaning we have in our mind for what scared us. When we think about rejection as another person's bad decision rather than a comment about us and how good we are, it is far easier to feel okay about being rejected. The key is to get okay with experiencing any and all of our fears so that we are free to do what we want to do.

Building Happiness into Your Mind

The pursuit of happiness is the main focus of the billion-dollar psychology and self-improvement industry. I believe we all have the ability to build happiness effectively into our minds. In doing so, you will ensure that you are in the best state possible to make great use of your time.

Since we know more about the brain than ever before, we understand that you can train your brain to release good feelings and create positive emotions through using our minds in new ways. Every time we think a thought, we make connections between neurons in our brain. The more we think these thoughts, the stronger those connections become and the more we develop this way of thinking as a habit.

In exploring the art of being happy, I have identified two primary types of happiness. Interestingly enough, I found a cultural and neurological difference between these two types. My slightly crude but easy to understand model is just a way of thinking about happiness, but I have found it very useful in helping people become happier.

The first type of happiness is the Western type of happiness, which involves concepts such as success, drive and achievement. It is the happiness we get from challenging ourselves and getting results. It is a feeling of pleasure and fulfilment that helps us feel good about how we are having an impact on the world. This feeling is linked quite directly to the feeling of motivation. We feel motivated and compelled to achieve more and get more of this good feeling.

As I previously mentioned, the chemical in our brains which most directly corresponds to this feeling is dopamine. It is the main chemical released when we experience pleasure or whenever we achieve a result.

The second type of happiness is the Eastern type of happiness, which involves concepts like contentment, enlightenment and satisfaction. It is the sense of being satisfied with ourselves and our lives and not needing to do anything in order to be happy. We are simply happy with where we are, what we have and who we are. Our contentment is not dependent on anything and so it is unconditional.

In our brains, the chemical which is linked to this is serotonin, which when released gives us a feeling of contentment. The interesting thing is that often, when we are releasing a large amount of dopamine, we seem to be releasing much less serotonin. Conversely, when we are high in serotonin levels we are not releasing as much dopamine. This makes sense, as when we are too dependent on outside achievements for a good feeling, we are not very content. Also, when we are too content, we are not very motivated or inspired to achieve anything.

Both types of happiness, I believe, are important to create. Western happiness is necessary because it ensures that we will be motivated and will contribute positively and successfully towards improving the world and our lives. Eastern happiness is crucial because I believe that we need to take control over our own brains so that we feel good even when the world isn't working like we want it to. Here are some tips to help you create both kinds of happiness.

Happy Time Tips

1 Set goals, motivate yourself and reward yourself for achieving the goals.

2 Create a gratitude book. Review all the great aspects of your life and all the things you have to feel grateful about.

3 Schedule in plenty of activities that you enjoy and that make you improve in new ways.

4 Schedule in meditation time where you can relax and feel good about your life.

5 List out everything you would like to get better at, learn more about it and take steps to do so.

6 Make a list of all the great personality qualities that you already possess.

Clarifying Language

Have you ever found yourself listening to someone who doesn't seem to have an "off" switch and spends their time telling you how important what they have to say is, yet when you try to find out what they are saying, you have really no idea?

So much time is wasted every day because of unclear communication, confusion and mixed messages. Language plays a pivotal role in helping you to save time through your communication. By learning how to become clearer with your language, you can ensure that you are maximising the time you do spend communicating with others.

In order for you to make sure your communication is as clear as possible, you need to make sure that it is simple, clear and precise. The way to do this is to utilise questions before you say whatever you have to say.

- Why am I saying what I am about to say?
- What do I want to say?
- What is the simplest way to say it?
- Is this exactly what I want to say?

Once you have answered these questions you will have a clearer understanding of the best way of communicating for you. Next, it is important to ask questions of those with whom you communicate.

- What is their understanding?
- Do they see it the way I see it?
- If not, how do they see it differently and how can I explain myself better?

It's also a good idea to clarify what other people are saying. You can do this by asking precise questions whenever you are speaking to others. These are questions that allow you to get more precise and specific information. Such questions include:

- How specifically?
- When specifically?
- Where exactly?
- Who exactly?
- What specifically?
- What exactly do you mean?

Four Keys to Efficient Communication

In order to communicate in the most effective and efficient way possible, it's worth bearing the following four keys in mind. Communication should be:

- **Relatable**
- **Relevant**
- **Memorable**
- **Concise**

Relatable

Sometimes it will be appropriate to use metaphors that make more sense to the other person. This will help them more quickly understand what you are talking about. If they are interested in sports, metaphors about goals and performance are more likely to help them understand you than discussing objectives and standards.

It's also a good idea to listen to the other person literally and use their key words back to them. This not only ensures that you are hearing what they say literally, but it also enables you to reflect back to them what they said, which makes them feel like you are on the same page as them.

People like those who make them feel good, so focus on making them feel good and you will have more of their attention and concentration and it will be easier to communicate successfully with them. This does not mean doing things always just to please others and certainly does not mean letting them walk all over you. It means that you are simply aware that whenever you make a person feel good, it is easier for them to relate to you. Appealing to their egos and letting them feel important are two effective ways of doing this.

- Listen to the terms and metaphors that others use.
- Create metaphors that are relatable for them.
- Use those terms and metaphors back to them.
- Make them feel good and valued when you are communicating with them.

Relevant

One factor that you need to be aware of is the context in which you find yourself communicating. You can give people concrete rather than abstract examples, which will help them make sense of what you are saying more easily. When explaining something to them, try to find relevant and useful examples that make your ideas easier to understand. When communicating with others, ask yourself questions like:

251

- How is this relevant to them?
- What is a good example I can give them to best illustrate this point?

Memorable

It's also important that you do your best to make your communication memorable. You can do this by attaching feelings to the ideas that you want them to remember. People remember what is associated with a strong emotional state.

People also tend to remember what is presented to them first and last. This is known in psychology as the **primacy** and **recency** effect. So ensure that you make the point you want them to get as the first point you make and the last point you make.

Whenever you have a presentation of some kind to do, ensure that the start of it captures attention, creates a strong positive feeling and makes an important point you want your audience to get.

With each presentation, also create a memorable ending which leaves your audience feeling good and reminds them of an important point. It's also a good idea to summarise your main points clearly and concisely.

When introducing your ideas or thoughts, tell your audience what you are planning on saying, then say it, and then tell them what you have told them.

Concise

There is a term called an "elevator pitch" which is often used in Hollywood. This is where a scriptwriter finds themselves standing next to a famous movie director or producer in a lift, and they have about 30 seconds to pitch an idea for a story.

This is a good way to look at our own communication. It's important to practise your ability to get your point across in a concise way. Mostly, we don't have enough time to explain ourselves as we would want to. So, we need to learn how to say what we want to say in a much shorter time.

Exercise

Elevator Pitch

1 Try writing out a paragraph of what you would like to say to someone.

2 Go through that paragraph and try to reduce it to one sentence without losing any meaning.

3 Try to convey the same message in the fewest words possible.

The Power of Positive Speaking

Research suggests that people who are happy, motivated, successful and flexible have a positive attitude. Since how you think is governed by how you speak, you can develop a positive attitude by taking charge of how you speak.

Now, while many negative thinkers believe that they are just naturally like that and can't change, that is simply an example of their negative attitude at work. The truth is that you can train yourself into developing a new, more useful attitude.

This is actually a simple process but it requires some conscious attention and awareness and enough discipline to change. It involves you paying attention to yourself when you hear yourself saying something negative after the word "but". The word "but" focuses all the attention of the listener on the part of the sentence that comes after it. So, most people who have a negative attitude will find that they are often saying something which could be positive and then immediately following that with "but" and a negative slant on everything.

The key is to change the sequence around so that, instead of starting with the positive and then using "but" and the negative, you start with the negative, use "but" and end with the positive.

This simple skill is something I have recommended earlier in Chapter 7 to help those who find themselves hesitating. I also taught it to one of the participants on the programme, Michael Gallagher, and he found himself dramatically changing his attitude over a couple of weeks simply by practising it. Michael initially worried a lot and saw the negative side to things. When he began to catch himself and make the adjustments asked of him, he found himself developing a new habit of seeing the brighter side of things because he was always finishing with a positive concept. This was evident in the change of his language from the start of the process to the very end.

For example, Michael said that he would give the technique a try but that it might not work. All I got him to do was to repeat it but with the sequence changed around. He then said that he wasn't sure if it would work but that he would give it a try. Instantly, he learned that his focus was now on the positive thought of giving it a try.

By simply paying attention to your language, you can find yourself actually being able to shift your entire attitude.

17

Creating Your New Schedule

"Planning is bringing the future into the present so that you can do something about it now."

ALAN LAKEIN

Creating your new schedule involves finding a way to capture events, tasks and actions in some sort of order in terms of when you would like to do them. This can be done with diaries, planners or calendars.

There are a wide variety of diaries available these days. You can get a paper diary in the form of a small hardback diary, an A5 diary or an A4 diary (the size of a refill pad) or a Filofax. You can get one with a page per day or two pages per week.

You can also get an electronic diary. You have the option of a diary on your computer, iPhone or Blackberry device. You can even synchronise your diaries on these different devices so that, when one changes, they all change. Whether you go electronic or with paper, the key is that you use something that works for you.

There are at least three different ways of tracking dates in your life – a diary, a calendar and a wall planner. Diaries keep track of what you are doing day-by-day, calendars track your activities each month while a wall planner lays out your events for the year.

You can also use these three systems to record where the members of your family will be and of any appointments you will have. You need to get into the habit of updating all three systems and keeping them all in synch with each other. Once you do that, you will ensure that you have a fail-proof system of recording your activities.

Now, I am fully aware that some people aren't a big fan of diaries. However, the key is to remember that they are simply a reminder to you of key events. There are so many different choices these days into how to organise your schedule. You need to find something that works for you.

Of course, it's not essential to have a diary, a calendar *and* a year planner. You should have one that outlines the month ahead, a few months ahead or a year ahead, if possible. I have a wall planner that marks out my year. I also have a diary that marks out the specifics of what I do each day. At the beginning of the diary I also have a mini wall planner which marks out the year as well. This means I have a way of tracking where I am wherever I go.

There is no correct way to schedule. There are only different ways that work for you in various circumstances. Your choice in how you schedule your time should ensure that you have a useful system which lets you know easily where you need to be, what you need to remember and what you need to do on particular dates and times.

Identify when you have the most amount of work to do and plan accordingly, so that you can schedule at times where you have more time available. This will ease the amount of work you have to do from day to day.

Having a clear and updated schedule makes everything you do and every decision you have to make so much easier. You can switch off more easily because you have something keeping track of your life for you. It is a wonderfully liberating and time-saving device.

Build Your Own Kind of Schedule

Find your own way of scheduling time. Become aware of the way you think about time and play around with different kinds of schedules until you find one that works for you. Do you find it easier to plan things when the months go from left to right or when they go from top to bottom? By establishing how you think about each day, week and month passing spatially in your mind, you can find a way of constructing a timetable and schedule which works with your brain in the most efficient way.

Whatever scheduling tool you use – Blackberry, laptop, etc. – the key is that they have a number of things in common. For daily tasks, it's important to avoid scheduling activities back to back. Often, in an attempt to get more done, we tend to try to fit in as much as possible and we end up with no time between appointments. It is essential to have some buffer between events so that we can reflect on the last activity and prepare for the next.

That way, it ensures that we are in an optimum state to perform at our best. This can be true of events that are on for a few days in a row. Make sure that you schedule days off and time where you can relax as well.

When you enter an item into a calendar or wall planner, write down the details and add tasks related to it. It's important to add such events as birthdays and other family occasions to it as well. That way, you are always on top of things.

Colour-code different events/activities so that you can spot from a distance what kind of activities are on and when. That way, it is also possible to see whether or not you have a good balance in your life. If you colour work events in red or black, and social events in green or yellow, a quick glance at your calendar will tell you whether or not you are making enough time for the things that matter.

Place the calendar/wall planner in one location in your home where you will look regularly. It's also a good idea to take your diary with you wherever you go. Each week, take five minutes just to make sure your diary and calendar/wall planner are synchronised.

Catching Up and Decluttering

It would be a silly assumption to suggest that you have nothing to catch up on, since you are reading this book. Of course, there may be projects that are not yet finished and tasks not yet completed. Some people have a tendency to think, "Well, I like all this time management stuff, so I will start it once I have caught up with everything else." Those kinds of thoughts will lead you to stagnation, as you will never fully catch up unless you start making the changes now.

What you have been reading about needs to be implemented immediately and not "when you are ready". The reason is because you need to put the new habits and disciplines in place so that you don't find yourself falling any further behind.

Catching up involves clearing the backlogs and getting a handle on what you need to do. This can be done quite simply. Once you go through and determine what you need to catch up on, the next step is to identify the specific steps that need to be taken and prioritise them. When you have done that, you will have a far clearer perspective on what you need to put in your diary. You can then include these tasks in your weekly or monthly schedule.

For example, many people find their inbox brimming with hundreds of emails. Take a few hours and dedicate it completely to email. Without checking for any new email every few minutes, spend all the time you can focusing on cleaning things up and organising your email so that it is easy to use.

Go through your email and respond to any emails you need to. Estimate seven different types of emails you get by topic and create folders for each of these email groups. Add an extra urgent email folder for anything that requires attention this week. This should be the folder you work from each day. Next, you can simply go through your inbox and decide whether to delete them, put them in the folder for attention this week or place them in one of the other seven folders. They should only be kept in the inbox if they require immediate attention within the next few hours.

This might take you a couple of hours but is well worth it in terms of the time it saves you looking for emails and tracking back conversations with people. This same process can be done with incoming post in the office. The object is to clean out the inbox tray and identify the various tasks that need to be done and when they need to be done.

At home, different areas of catch-up might include paying bills or ordering DVDs or even something as basic as washing-up or laundry. In Section 7, I'll offer some suggestions which may prove valuable in these different areas. For now, the key would be to establish what needs to be done and immediately factor it into your 4Ds System.

The object is not necessarily to catch up immediately but to create a plan whereby you will be able to catch up pretty soon with everything. It is fitting your catching up into the plan.

It will also be important to ensure that the various systems you have are organised as efficiently as possible. This means that you can check the way in which you will deal with tasks, activities and information in the future and ensure that you are able to deal with everything more smoothly and effectively when it comes along. There is no point in catching up and then creating just as big a mess with the same tired old ways of doing things. Figure out a way that will work best for you and start using it consistently.

Building a new system will obviously depend what you are trying to do. A system of organising emails could be done as described above. Activities like cleaning would require you to dedicate a regular period of time to it on a consistent basis to ensure that things don't fall too much behind. If it's a project for college or studies for an exam, it is important that once you complete the project you make some time available for regular revision so you can be on top of your work at all times.

Regarding **clutter**, even though some people thrive in untidiness, most people find that their productivity suffers as a result of clutter. When you are surrounded by chaos and your work space feels as if it is a bomb site, it may well be necessary to clear away the mess and allow yourself room to see things more clearly. Of course, there is a saying: "If a cluttered desk is the sign of a cluttered mind, what is an empty desk the sign of?" But more than this, we must learn to adopt a balance between the two. Having an organised working environment means that you can have a clearer perspective on the different tasks you are to do.

Tidying is not the same as decluttering. Decluttering means identifying the objects and papers and things that are scattered about and putting them in their rightful place as well as finding things which are superfluous and unnecessary and throwing them out.

The Art of Effective Planning

Becoming effective at planning means that you think things out more clearly. Real planning is all about having a goal and deciding how you are going to achieve that goal. What steps are you going to take in what order to allow you to achieve that goal? Planning is a simple skill but is crucial for the good management of your time and life.

It's important that you don't plan too little and don't plan too much. When you plan too little, then you may find yourself not accounting for everything and thus you might become stuck without what you need. When you plan too much, you can sometimes start hesitating as you overthink things and attempt to make everything perfect.

Also, planning is different to preparing. Preparing is when you have a task to do and you implement the part of the plan in which you get ready to do the task. So, you factor in preparing as a part of any good plan.

So, how do you plan?

How to Plan

- Establish **goals and actions** required
- Establish **people** needed
- Establish **resources** needed

A good plan answers the following questions:

Establish Goals and Actions Needed:

- What do you want to achieve?
- What will you need to have done in order to achieve that?
- What needs to have happened for that to happen?
- How much time do you need?
- What are all the actions that need to take place in order for this plan to be successful?
- What sequence do these actions need to be performed in?

Establish People Needed:

- Whose help do you need?
- Which people are involved?
- How can you get them involved and helping?
- When will you do that?
- What specifically do you need them to do?

Establish Other Resources Needed:

- What resources do you need?
- How can you get them?
- When will you do that?
- How will you use them?

Now, once you have successfully answered these questions, the next step is to examine these answers and create a project "to-do" list where you divide each item you must do into smaller actions. Then, you can specify when you are going to complete each smaller task. To break this down ask yourself the following questions:

- What are the main actions required in this plan?
- What are the things that need to be done in order for this action to be fully completed?

When defining how long each action will take you, it's important to give yourself tight deadlines to start with. Deadlines are important in order for you to maximise your chances of success. There is a law in psychology known as Parkinson's Law, which suggests that a task expands to fit the time available. What this means is that whatever amount of time you give yourself to do something will be the amount of time it takes you for that particular activity. For example, if you give yourself an hour to do something and you get it done, you would take close to three hours to get it done if you gave yourself three hours.

KEY POINT

The length of time you spend on a task will expand depending on the time available

---

Three Important Qualities of Any Plan

Any good plan should have three extra qualities. You need to organise a reward system that keeps you motivated and disciplined. You need to build in buffer time, as no plan ever goes perfectly. You need to develop flexibility in the plan and prepare for both foreseen and unforeseen consequences.

Reward System

Once you have described the various steps of your plan and what you need to be doing, the next step is to identify a certain amount of steps that you will complete and decide on a **reward** that you will give yourself once you have completed those steps by the specified deadline.

Give yourself regular rewards for each main part of the plan that you implement and take time to review the reasons why you are doing it. This will ensure that you are on track and fully motivated.

Build in Buffer Time

When you are creating the schedule to your plan, make sure you have a few extra days free, as it is nearly impossible to be entirely accurate in your estimates of how long an entire project will take to do. Also, because it is rare for everything to go to plan, it's essential to have contingency plans and extra time in hand to deal with whatever issues arise.

It's necessary to be aware of a principle called **delay discounting**. This occurs when we perceive that we have more slack time in the future than we actually have. We have a much better ability to gauge how much money we will need but, when it comes to time, it's harder to estimate, because of the intangible nature of time in the mind.

Furthermore, research suggests that our estimations on how long something will take us to do are far less accurate than our estimations on how long something will take others to do. It is a good idea to think about the length of time something will take from the perspective of how long it would take someone else.

Develop Flexibility in the Plan

Developing **flexibility** in the plan simply involves identifying the potential problems that may arise in your efforts to carry out the plan. Take some time before you begin and ask the question: What are the potential difficulties that may arise in carrying out the plan?

Incorporate contingency plans in there as well. Planning for different scenarios is a very important and useful step that will allow you to respond much more effectively to whatever happens.

Once you have identified these challenges, use the buffer time you have allocated to sort out and deal with these challenges. Also, during the course of the plan, if you are faced with an unforeseen challenge, again use the buffer time to deal with it.

Exercise

The Planner's Time Machine

1 An effective way of planning is to visualise the action you need to take having been completed. You can do this in the following way.

2 Imagine vividly in your mind having successfully completed the task.

3 From this point of time in the future look back into the past and examine the steps you took towards achieving the results you achieved.

4 Feel the pride and satisfaction of having been successful and remember from this point how you effectively completed each of the steps of the plan.

5 Write down the various steps that you imagined in this visualisation.

Any good plan requires that you carry it out with motivation and determination. The plan of action that I give to each of the participants in the *Not Enough Hours* programme is no different. In the next section, we will examine more closely how this plan of action works and how you can actualise the changes you have begun to make.

SECTION 6

ACTUALISE

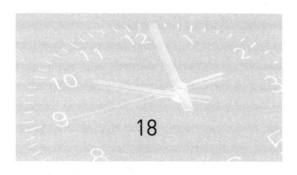

18

A Time to Change

"We are what we repeatedly do. Excellence, therefore, is not an act but a habit."

ARISTOTLE

Once you have analysed what you have been doing, prioritised what's most important and organised yourself in new and more efficient and productive ways, you will be well on your way to achieving the kind of life you want and deserve.

In this final part of the TimeWise system, let's take a closer look at how you can immediately implement the ideas from this book in your life. I want to examine the elements of change, motivation and discipline, and explore what will ensure that you can apply the ideas from the book successfully to your life. In this section, you will also learn how to create your own action plan.

Doctors I have worked with have often told me that their biggest challenge is getting people to take their medication. This is an issue of motivation, of course, but it is something that all those involved in helping people to change their habits have to face. The truth, of course, is that you can never guarantee that they will change. You can only make it more likely by doing your best to motivate them as well as you can.

Someone once said to me that the *Not Enough Hours* programme would be challenging for me, since it would examine whether or not what I did actually worked. To me, that is way off the mark. You see, I know that what I do works, like a carpenter knows that a hammer and nails work. The question is not about whether the time management ideas work but whether or not people actually use them.

I have a saying I like to repeat when I am teaching courses. If you do it, it will work. If you don't do it, science has shown undeniably that it won't work. Actualising means putting ideas into practice. It means taking the systems and principles and techniques and bringing them into the way you do things. The key is, if you do so, your life and time will be far better managed and you'll find more time and better quality time available. If you don't . . . you won't.

Often, what we decide to do and what we actually do are two very different things. I constantly meet people who tell me that they "know" what to do but for some reason they just can't do it. Also, for some reason, they seem to be trapped and unable to help themselves. Along comes an expert who will save the day for them and get them to do it. But the important thing to remember here is that they are still the ones who must do it. In order for your life to change, *you* must change it. It's not as difficult as people may think it is, but it requires awareness and deliberate, constant and disciplined action.

There is an important principle in psychology called the "self-fulfilling prophecy". What this means is that often we will make true whatever beliefs we have, by acting in certain ways to prove them as true. So, when we believe something, we will act based upon those beliefs. Our actions will in turn create results which are more likely to confirm our beliefs. For example, suppose we believe we are a "late person". That belief causes us to be late, which then confirms to us our belief that we are a "late person".

The key to using this is to become aware of any of our beliefs about time and lateness that are not useful. Once we do so, we can challenge such beliefs and ask ourselves what we would like to believe instead. Then we can act in accordance with those new, more useful beliefs, which will create results that will confirm the new beliefs to us.

One of the beliefs we need to act from is the belief that change can be simple and quick. Many people believe the opposite. But unless you change this belief, you may be facing a long, hard road. When you start to believe and act as if change is simple and quick, you will find yourself being able to prove this as true.

Sometimes it can seem harder to get ourselves to do something than to get other people to do it. By looking at your life, taking part in the exercises I outline and realising how important these changes are to you, I'm hoping that

273

you will take the steps necessary to succeed with your plan of action.

Time for a Big Change

Before focusing on the more detailed areas of your life that you are re-evaluating, it's a good idea that you take a general look at your life and examine whether or not you are wasting your time and your life doing something which you don't want to do.

If you are in a job that you dislike or that bores you, that is a big waste of time. Since we spend so much time in work, it is vital that you make sure you enjoy what you do. Similarly, being in a relationship that you don't want to be in is another big waste of time. Of course, I am not suggesting if you don't like your job or relationship, then pack it in, as perhaps time will change your mind, or indeed a shift in attitude might do it. What I am suggesting is that if you have found yourself continuously down as a result of doing what you are doing or who you are with, you have to think carefully about whether or you want to spend your time there.

There are many reasons why people stay in circumstances that they don't like. However, if you are staying in them out of a fear of change, rejection, loneliness or failure, then that's not useful. Decisions should be made based upon what you want and what is the right thing to do, not on what scares you.

Changing Your Brain

Whenever you build a new habit and replace an old one, you are literally rewiring your brain. Habits work in the brain by the connections we make. Our brains are constantly changing and adapting. This is known as "neuroplasticity".

Fundamentally, our brains are made up of millions of tiny nerve cells called neurons. These neurons connect to each other through bridges called synapses. Each time you think a thought or engage in a behaviour, your brain sends signals across many of these synapses between neurons. The more you practise this habit, the stronger these bridges become and the connection becomes quicker and more automated. That's why practice causes improvement.

When you stop engaging in a habit, you are stopping your brain from sending the chemicals across the same synapses. The less you send them across, the weaker the connection becomes. Then, when you replace that behaviour with a new habit and you practise the new habit you will, once again, be sending chemical signals across bridges, which will gradually make the new habit stronger, faster and more automated. Thus, your brain will learn a new habit.

Six Reasons Why People Don't Change

So, what is it that holds people back from actually following through on the changes that they know they need to make? I've identified six reasons why people don't change.

1 Fear of Change
2 Bad Habits
3 Lack of Focus
4 Lack of Motivation
5 Lack of Clarity
6 Lack of Certainty

Reason 1: Fear of Change

The first reason why people don't change is that they fear change. The *idea* of a change, of course, is promising but they ultimately know that there is a lot of uncertainty and this requires toil, which comes with change. Change is not always welcome in their lives, which is revealed by the old adage "The devil you know is better than the devil you don't".

When you are unsure about the future, you can be unsure that the decision that you made to improve was a good one. By second-guessing yourself and fretting over the decision you made, you can end up in a stagnant rut which is challenging to get out of.

In order to overcome this fear, you need to own up to it and learn more about the potential dangers of change. Then, learn about the potential dangers of staying the same and in the same old rut. Often, it's about leverage – making sure that you have a good enough reason to change. You can also find ways of making the change seem a lot less like change. Frame it as an improvement, which suggests building on what you are already doing.

To become more certain about the results of your changes, it is a great idea to bring your goals through the "well-formed goals" exercise described earlier. This will lead you to examine whether or not these goals are really "worth" achieving. Discovering your goals and priorities ensures that you will become clear over how your life will be affected by the changes that you make.

Sometimes people prevent themselves from changing in an effort to sabotage the process because of fear. They fear the potential failure or success of the change. If things change, the uncertainty of the new kind of life scares them. If things don't change, the miserable feeling of having failed scares them.

Take Michael Gallagher as an example; fear of failure was the real reason he wouldn't start a course in sports coaching, even though he initially used excuses about time and money. Once he confronted this fear and realised that failure was not as big a deal as he realised, he felt confident enough to take on the course.

Reason 2: Bad Habits

Bad habits around time are habits that keep us repeating actions which unnecessarily waste time instead of doing the things we need to do. Bad habits take a little while to identify, but once we do so, we can readily eliminate them. Pay attention to where these habits occur and then find out if they serve any other purpose. Sometimes, a smoking break is an opportunity to spend social time with friends. Other times, as Freud pointed out "a cigar is only a cigar". Once you know the intention of the bad time habits, you need to address them. When you have done this, it is then essential that you practise the new behaviour as often as possible to build it into a new habit.

Reason 3: Lack of Focus

Often people find themselves beginning to get stuck into a new set of behaviours but they get sidetracked by constant interruptions that take their attention away from the new habits they are supposed to be practising. Being able to change focus from one

277

thought to another is a useful skill in many contexts. The problem comes when our lack of constant attention allows us to slip back into non-useful habits and patterns.

Getting yourself to focus on the different aspects of the changes that you are making ensures that you will be incorporating your wandering tendency in a way that works for you. Also, asking questions which direct and focus the mind is a good idea. Questions like the following can help you keep on track:

- What exactly do I need to remember to do now to ensure I have the life I want?

- What is my priority right now?

Reason 4: Lack of Motivation

A lack of motivation is another huge factor which influences whether or not we engage in the new behaviours. Unless we are sufficiently motivated, any change we make will not last very long. It is essential to feel motivated and compelled towards achieving our goals in order for us to make the appropriate changes positively.

Reason 5: Lack of Clarity

Being unclear about what it is that we are supposed to do or why we are doing it is something else which can prevent us from maintaining a new change programme. We need to understand exactly what it is that we are doing to allow ourselves become as disciplined as possible about it.

Reason 6: Lack of Responsibility

Another reason people sometimes don't change is because they fail to take responsibility for their problems or for the solution. The psychological area of attribution examines how human beings often attribute negative behaviours and intentions to others more quickly than to themselves, while the opposite is true for positive behaviours and intentions.

We are quick to rationalise our own behaviours and slow to do so for the behaviours of others. We blame outside influences for our failures and come up with creative excuses as to why we can't change. This leaves us with the problem always looming because it is protected by a wealth of excuses.

You can overcome this lack of responsibility by recognising the real problem and being honest with yourself. Instead of getting caught up in blame or finding out the deep-seated reason why you have developed the behaviour or way of thinking that isn't useful, focus on a different question. Ask: "How can I take control over my mind and behaviour to change things around?" When you ask that question, you will start the process of change.

Facing the consequences of your old behaviour and changing the way you were thinking about it will help you enormously to turn things around. When you decide to change and you realise that you hold the keys to doing so yourself, you free yourself from the constraint of excuses and you find it easier to make changes last.

Seven Reasons Why You CAN Change

Of course, just as there are reasons why people don't change, there are also reasons why people do change and reasons why you can change. Conveniently, I have found seven. If you use the following ideas, you will change.

1 Movement

2 Clarity

3 Accountability

4 Reward

5 Motivation

6 Discipline

7 Identity

Reason 1: Movement – You get yourself moving in the right direction

Have you ever found yourself going to the gym for a couple of weeks, almost every day, feeling determined to become the fittest person in the universe? Then you miss a couple of days and you find it impossible to get back there. It is easy to relate to this, especially with things like New Year's resolutions.

Many people have a tendency to change things in big sweeping movements. Through "binge changes", they attempt to change a lot, immediately. This often doesn't work as effectively as desired, as we don't always keep them up like we can do.

Instead, it is important to ensure that we keep our actions consistent. This means that we make a number of changes to our behaviour and continuously remind ourselves of these changes. It may be as simple as learning to compile a "to-do" list for the next day the night before but we keep this up each evening. The trick is to make the new habits fit into your daily and evening routine. Get started and get stuck in. That will get you moving and it's always easier from there on in.

Reason 2: Clarity – You have a clear roadmap to success

The next reason why we are able to change is that we have a clear roadmap of where we need to go, what we need to do and what we need to achieve and by when. An example of this is having an action plan.

By ensuring that we know what we need to do and by understanding how to overcome any challenges in our way, we can ensure that we remain on top of things. The exercises in the Prioritise section should help you with this.

Reason 3: Accountability – You make yourself accountable for the change

Another step to making changes effectively is to set a deadline for the change and to create consequences for yourself that will arise if you do not succeed. You may have noticed that people seem well able to make getting fit into a habit when they have an event coming up such as an important competition, marathon or wedding. The fact that they have some sort of event which will establish their accountability is a great motivator for them. Once you create such an event, however, the next step is to ensure that you have reasons to keep things up. After a while, your new habit will become a natural behaviour, as long as you stay consistent.

You can also add more stakes to changing. For example, make deals with your friends and offer to buy dinner if you are late for meeting them. Suggest to your children next time you say that you can't make a cinema trip that you will take a full day off work in return. There are plenty of ways to set things up so that you stack up consequences of drifting from your plan.

Reason 4: Reward – You reward yourself for progress made

Another factor that can help change along is ensuring that you reward yourself for any progress you make. This means giving yourself rewards whenever you achieve one of the sub-goals on the way to the final achievement. Breaking things down makes things easier to achieve. Rewards work best if they are consistent but irregular. In other words, vary the kind of rewards and the timing of rewards for yourself so that it keeps you working hard to achieve results.

Changing habits successfully is about developing a different attitude, paying attention to yourself, setting goals and rewarding yourself every time you change your behaviour. The more you do this, the more you train your body into new behavioural patterns.

Reason 5: Motivation – You know why you are changing

There's an old saying that goes: "If you have a big enough 'why', you can find any 'how'." Understanding why we are changing is a vital part of ensuring that we do what we need to do in order to change. The reason for our change must be two-sided. It must be because of what we want to achieve in our life as well as what we don't want in our life.

Reason 6: Discipline – You are disciplined to do whatever is required

The difference between those who keep at a new activity and those who don't are that when both groups find themselves not in the mood to do it, those who are disciplined do it anyway and therefore keep at it.

As well as being motivated towards doing things differently, it is vital to understand the importance of being disciplined and being able to push yourself towards doing what you know you need to do regardless of how you feel at the time. When you know what you have to do and you know how to do it, the step towards doing it is about disciplining yourself towards taking action.

Reason 7: Identity – You commit the change to become who you are

You must also make sure that your new behaviours become part of who you are. Many people who try to stop smoking, for example, go back on the cigarettes with the excuse: "I'm a smoker." You need to ensure that you start seeing yourself as being the kind of person who exhibits the new behaviours as a habit.

So, if you are starting to give yourself more time to get ready and making a real effort to be early for events when before you were late, you need to see it as something that is a part of who you are. You need to see yourself as the kind of person who is early for things. This switch in identity doesn't need to happen overnight but it does need to happen before you have safely made the changes and new habits permanent.

It's also an idea to ask yourself the question: "what do I need to do in order to fully committ to these changes?" People generally have different perspectives on what a commitment involves. The action plan is one way of getting you to commit yourself to doing things differently. Ask yourself what other ways you can ensure that you commit yourself.

The final three of these seven reasons for change – motivation, discipline and identity – are particularly important. Let's look at them more closely.

The Power of Motivation

Motivation is the drive we all have to do something. It works upon the principles of pleasure and pain. We are motivated from what we have to gain, which gives us pleasure. We are also motivated from what we have to lose, which gives us pain.

One way of motivating yourself is by imagining what will happen if you achieve your goals and use your time in the best possible way. When you vividly imagine this, you will feel drawn towards it.

You can also imagine the worst case scenario which might happen if you do not make the necessary changes you need to make and make that vivid also. This allows you to intensify what is at stake in your change process.

Some people like to plan and some don't. Instead they prefer just to deal with the world as it happens. Now, of course, it is useful if we have some kind of plan for the future, but if you don't like planning, you don't have to fixate on this. Some people are better motivated by implementing a new plan to change. They will be more effective when they proactively plan how they are going to change things and when. Others are better motivated when they focus on just tailoring their responses reactively in new ways to deal with the world differently. So they are more likely to adapt their behaviours so that they deal with things more effectively than before. In reality, they plan to respond to the world as it comes. They react to it in a new way which helps them have more time. The idea is to work to your strengths.

Another key to motivation is how you structure what you have to do. Often, when a task is perceived as being too big, it can be daunting enough to remove some of the motivation for people to do it. When you break the task down into smaller parts, it makes it easier to feel motivated to do it.

Motivation Exercise

1 Think about something you want to be more motivated to do. Why do you want to achieve this result?

2 What will you see, hear and feel when you have achieved this result? How will it positively affect your life?

3 What will happen if you don't take the actions necessary to achieve this result?

4 Whether you like planning or responding, imagine yourself doing what you need to do and getting the results.

5 Reward yourself for the actions you take towards achieving the result.

6 Break down a task into smaller parts so you can see yourself accomplishing it more easily.

Making a New Year Resolution into a New Year Reality: The Power of Motivational Language

Every year it's the same. We say to ourselves, I really should start that new exercise regime for the New Year. I should stop smoking. I should eat better. Should, should, should. But it never seems to make a difference. After a less-than-valiant effort, we find ourselves back at square one, wondering if we will ever manage to finally do what we know is important for us to do.

An essential element involved in structuring your time more effectively is in your use of motivational language. From the personal development tool NLP (Neuro-Linguistic Programming), we can learn clever ways of using words to motivate ourselves in more powerful ways.

The trick to this comes in how we declare a vow to change what we have. Consider the following sentences. Repeat each of them to yourself and notice how you feel after saying it. How likely are you to actually follow through on the commitment after each sentence?

- *I **can** be on time in the future.*
- *I **could** be on time in the future.*
- *I'd **like** to be on time in the future.*
- *I **want** to be on time in the future.*
- *I **should** be on time in the future.*
- *I **have to** be on time in the future.*
- *I **need to** be on time in the future.*
- *I **must** be on time in the future.*
- *I **will** be on time in the future.*
- *I **am going** to be on time in the future.*

Try each sentence again but in this instance replace the phrase "on time" with whatever action you wish to take in the future. Which ones work for you? Which sentences seem to work better in motivating you? Some of the sentences might make you feel restricted or annoyed and others give you a sense of freedom, but the real question is, which sentences make you more likely to actually do it?

It is different for different people but if you can find which sentence works for you and what tone of voice you use to say that sentence, you will find the key that unlocks the heart of your motivation. The words that make these sentences different are known as motivational words. By using the right one, you can unlock your motivation. Also ensure that you use the tone of voice that works for you as well.

Exercise
Motivating Language

1　Go through the list above and find out which words work best for you and get you to take action.

2　Become aware of what tone of voice you use when you say the words that work, when they work.

3　Each time you are trying to motivate yourself to do something, use the same words as above and the same tone of voice that works for you. Notice how much more motivated you feel.

The Keys to Discipline

I describe discipline as the drive to continue to do something. This is different to motivation as, to me, discipline needs to become something that happens automatically. When we are disciplined, we perform the necessary actions without even thinking.

This is when we go to the gym even when we don't feel like going; when we say no to a cigarette even though we crave it; when we eat a piece of fruit instead of an ice cream after dinner. They are the choices that don't even feel like choices. We are doing them because we have developed a habit of doing them based upon the earlier choices and decisions we have made.

We can build discipline by considering how truly important the decisions we make to do something or not are. When you commit to the changes you wish to make and you decide on it 100 per cent, the next key is to foresee any possible problems that might prevent you from doing it and to make sure that you know how to overcome them.

When you foresee problems and you see yourself continuing with the new behaviours regardless of these issues, it will allow you to become disciplined in your actions.

Discipline Exercise

1 Think about the various tasks you perform every day, like brushing your teeth.

2 Notice when you think about this everyday task how you picture it in your mind.

3 Decide the specific action that you must take in order for you to get the results you want to get.

4 Be very clear about what the action is and what it will involve.

5 Imagine yourself doing it automatically in the same way you pictured the everyday task.

6 Imagine yourself engaging in everyday tasks and include this new action in the various tasks.

7 Leave reminders of the action if necessary. Make them impossible to miss. You could leave stickers on the fridge, notes on the coffee table or index cards in your car.

8 Follow through and do the action without any hesitation. Get straight into it. Get used to doing it this way.

Changing Your Identity

In order for you to manage your life successfully, the first questions you must ask yourself are: "Who am I?" and "Who do I want to be?" The key to long-lasting, permanent change is contained within the notion of identity.

Your identity reflects how you see yourself, how you think about yourself and what you feel about yourself. In psychology, these three concepts can be known as **self-image**, **self-concept** and **self-esteem**.

The images you make about yourself and the way you talk to yourself about yourself determine your self-image and self-concept while the way you treat yourself determines your self-esteem or how you feel about yourself.

Who you think you are will determine whether or not the changes you make to your behaviour will take hold or not. Often, when I work with somebody, I will get them to become completely comfortable with the new behaviours that I am suggesting. You have to ensure that your identity is consistent with whatever new behaviour you engage in.

For example, when I worked with Olivia, I asked her about the notion of scattiness. I pointed out that there were plenty of examples of cute, scatty girls who were the romantic heroes of some popular movies. Meg Ryan and Drew Barrymore are two actresses who typically play such scatty figures. Scattiness can be seen as a desirable trait.

What I wanted to know with Olivia was whether or not she might hold the notion of scattiness in some affection as a personality trait. When it was clear that she didn't, it was easier to be sure that she would be able to take the new behaviour of being well-organised and make it become a part of who she was. If she had wanted to remain scatty, then it was very possible that any change that she made would not have lasted very long as she would have reverted back to being scatty again.

Similarly, if you see yourself as a smoker, then no matter how hard you try, you will never be able to quit for good. The reason for this is very simple. Being a smoker is part of your identity. When it is who you are, you will always return to that person, no matter what you do differently.

One lady I worked with managed to make this change and it helped her stop smoking. She had tried everything but as she explained nothing worked because she was a smoker. I asked her how many cigarettes she smoked per day. She said 20. I asked her how long each cigarette took to smoke. She said four minutes.

I asked her the following question: if she was doing something for 22 hours and 40 minutes every day and something else for one hour and 20 minutes per day, which activity would she use to describe what kind of person she was? She smiled and understood what I was getting at. As soon as she saw herself as a non-smoker who smoked for an hour and twenty minutes a day, it was so much easier for her to quit.

We are not our behaviours but because we often describe ourselves in this way, then the trick is to engage in new behaviours.

The Power of Your Identity

Your identity is not who you are. It is who you think you are. We all base our identity on our conclusions about ourselves, which we extract from our experiences. The problem with this is that we will gather very different understandings about ourselves depending on what our beliefs are.

We develop ideas about the kind of people that we are. We then tend to look for evidence to prove these ideas are true. It is like we have a thinker and a "prover" in our minds. The thinker creates ideas that we have and our "prover" attempts to prove these ideas as being true.

Suppose someone tells us that we are not musical; we then search for every example we find and we use that as evidence to prove their conclusion correct. We discount and dismiss evidence to the contrary. If we get evidence of our potential skill in music, we might explain it away as being unique and not representative of the truth.

This explains why it is vital to develop an identity which fits with how you want to be in terms of time. If you believe that you are a "late person" then it will be an immense struggle for you to be on time whenever you have an event to attend. If on the other hand you realise that you are not a "late person" but that in the past you have been late often, then you can more easily decide to be on time or be early in the future. Because it is behaviour, you have control over it.

There are many examples where we allow our behaviours to become our identity but it is very important that we learn to separate the two when the combination is not useful.

The most useful way of thinking about your identity is to think of yourself as you are at your absolute best. When you think about yourself at your very best, you find yourself building a more resourceful and useful identity, which can allow you to make any appropriate changes to your behaviour easily.

So, when you are asking the question, "Who am I?", the key is to write out what kind of person you thought you were. Then, go through each quality you gave yourself and identify the behaviour you are talking about. For example, if you were to use the example, "I am a late person", change it to "I have been late for many events". By making it something you *do* rather than something you *are*, you have control over it. You can then finish with "I am a good person who has the ability to change any behaviour including this one and with a bit of effort I can be early and on time for everything from now on."

By going through this process, you will find yourself feeling differently about all the changes you are about to make. You will start seeing yourself as a person who is in control over your life and who balances the different activities and responsibilities of your life in effective and successful ways.

You can do this by visualising yourself using all the new strategies and techniques of life management that you have learnt in this book. Next, you can think about yourself as being well in control of every hour you spend. It's essential to think about yourself as someone who handles time brilliantly and with great discipline. This will involve you building new beliefs about who you are.

If you see yourself as a workaholic, then the danger is you will get lost in that description and it will remain who you are. The personality tendencies of Section 2 are just a description of behaviour and not an everlasting definition of who these "types" are.

When Conor changed his perspective on work, he remained a "hard worker" but he was no longer a "workaholic". This was an important switch. Seeing himself as a hard worker but primarily as a Dad and a husband allowed him quite powerfully to incorporate the new lifestyle changes into his life. He still works hard, but has learned to separate his work and home life more distinctively and therefore is spending more quality time at home with his family.

Oftentimes, we define ourselves by our job – I'm a "psychologist", or a "teacher" or an "entrepreneur". The identity of whatever roles you wish to engage in more often should start becoming your identity. You should see a valuable difference between what you have been doing and who you are.

Changing your Identity

Answer the following questions:

1 What kind of person are you in relation to time? Are you organised/unorganised, punctual/late, a time friend/ time stranger, motivated/lazy, a strong person/ a walkover? Write out a number of sentences about who you are starting with "I am . . ."

2 Go through each sentence and rephrase it in terms of behaviour in the past. So instead of "I am unorganised", change it to "I have behaved in an unorganised way in the past".

3 Write out what new behaviours you are going to engage in instead of the old behaviours in the future.

When you follow the steps above in describing your identity, detaching the behaviours from yourself, the next step is to start creating a new identity for yourself.

Who Do You Want to Be?

It's imperative to open up the scope of that description and start creating more ways of seeing yourself. You could see yourself as a parent or friend but when you do this, do not just see yourself, for example, as a parent who is like a mini-slave to your children. As a parent, the image should be of you caring for and being cared for by your children. It should be a broad and positive definition of "parent" that you hold inside your head, not just consisting of your responsibilities but also of how you want to be known. Ask yourself the following questions:

Exercise

Present Self

- Who are you?

- Who else are you?

- What are your roles and responsibilities?

- How are you known to the different people in your life?

As we have seen already, the importance of your identity cannot be underestimated. The way you think about yourself allows you to externalise old patterns of behaviour that caused you problems with time, and internalise new patterns of behaviour that help you to think differently about time.

Once you know who you think you are, the question is, who do you want to be? What kind of person with what kind of qualities? In order for you to maintain the changes required to free up your time and allow you to make the most of any moment, you must make changes at this identity level.

Exercise

Best Self

- Who are you at your absolute best?

- Who do you want to be?   .

- What kind of person with what kind of qualities?

- How do you want to be known to the different people in your life?

- What kind of person will you be when you have mastered using time in the most effective way?

It is not just a case of you doing new things; they must become a part of who you are. The key is to remind yourself of the answers to these questions over and over again. By reading and imagining what you have written down, you are telling your brain how to think about yourself.

Creating a TimeWise Self-Image

Here is a simple technique to help you start to see yourself as someone in control of your time and life.

- Take some of the biggest challenges you have with regards to time.

- Imagine the new you handling them brilliantly, with a clever and clear ability to manage your time more successfully. See yourself vividly, as you would be at your best, dealing with every challenge and issue easily. Imagine it as clearly and as vividly as you can.

- Step inside that self of yours and imagine what it feels like to be in control. Notice how the experience feels as if you were there, as if it was real. Imagining it as real will make it as real as it needs to be. The more you practise seeing yourself in this way, the more you will build potential for you to become the person that you desire to be.

Once you are ready to truly sign up and make things happen for yourself, then it's time to create your very own action plan.

19

Lights, Camera, Action

*"I have been impressed with the urgency of doing.
Knowing is not enough; we must apply. Being willing is
not enough; we must do."*

LEONARDO DA VINCI

Since taking responsibility is an essential part of making a change in your life, it's important to have a **plan of action** for yourself to carry out that reminds you of what you need to do and keep doing as you make those changes.

How to Create Your Own Plan of Action

The plan of action proved to be a popular and useful exercise that we employed in the *Not Enough Hours* show. The idea was simple. In order to ensure that each person continued on the road to personal change, it would be smart to create a plan for them to follow that could remind them of the most important things to focus on. An example of an action plan drawn up for one of the participants in the series is shown on the next page.

ACTION:
KEEP NEW PRIORITIES

Schedule in Family Time.
Home 4:30pm each day and most weekends off
Balance...any extra work...extra family time

WHEN:
Family Time Scheduled in Every Week.
For every day you are home after 7, you schedule an activity with family.

OVERCOMING POTENTIAL PROBLEMS:

POTENTIAL PROBLEM:
My workload gets so much and I feel I need to come in on a weekend to tackle it.

SOLUTION:
You decide to go in for four hours early on a Saturday making sure the full day is free for a family activity.

POTENTIAL PROBLEM:
Someone calls with a conference on both days of the weekend.

SOLUTION:
You ask yourself if you really need to do it. If yes, you balance family time. If not, you use an alternative

POTENTIAL PROBLEM:
You slip up and find yourself making an exception.

SOLUTION:
Take stock of what is happening, how important change is and what you need to do and do it.

ACTION:
SWITCH OFF

Have written down all tasks on to do list
Shut Down Office & Leave Laptop There
Use Golfing Strategy

WHEN:
Every Evening when finished at scheduled stop time.
When Leaving Office to Arrive Home.

OVERCOMING POTENTIAL PROBLEMS:

POTENTIAL PROBLEM:
People call you on your Mobile Phone after hours.

SOLUTION:
Divert the phone to the office so that you can only take text messages from family and friends.

POTENTIAL PROBLEM:
You get the DT's (Withdrawal Symptoms) from not being able to have the laptop at home.

SOLUTION:
You replace the laptop with activities at home so you are not just at home, you are doing something too.

POTENTIAL PROBLEM:
You wake up in the middle of the night with an idea.

SOLUTION:
You write the basic idea down in your notepad and schedule in time to expand on it.

ACTION:
DEALING WITH WORK

Keep In Tray Relevant with Immediate Tasks
Everything Else: Defer, Delete or Delegate.
Use a to-do task list & 4 Quadrants

WHEN:
Every morning when you come in and every evening when you leave keep an eye on the work.
Each week make a check on Quadrant Percentage.

OVERCOMING POTENTIAL PROBLEMS:

POTENTIAL PROBLEM:
You find your in tray is starting to overflow with tasks.

SOLUTION:
You go through the in tray and only keep in it what needs to be done that day and do it. Defer the rest.

POTENTIAL PROBLEM:
Someone gets talking to you at the office or at a conference and doesn't stop.

SOLUTION:
You ask yourself 'What is the purpose of the conversation and how can I achieve it quickly?'

POTENTIAL PROBLEM:
Someone asks you for help with something but you already have promised your family something.

SOLUTION:
You remember the most important people to you in life and make sure that they are not let down.

ACTION:
MAKE BUSINESS BETTER

Get New Software & Server
Hire the Right People & Delegate
Organising Workload More Efficiently

WHEN:
In the next week.
In the next month.
Every day keep to the disciplines.

OVERCOMING POTENTIAL PROBLEMS:

POTENTIAL PROBLEM:
Too much organisation scares you.

SOLUTION:
You balance it by being more impulsive with your family and make home time even more appealing.

POTENTIAL PROBLEM:
You find yourself resorting to pottering around office.

SOLUTION:
You re-evaluate what is important and not urgent and you get those things done.

POTENTIAL PROBLEM:
You find yourself double checking email or re-doing a job that is not yours.

SOLUTION:
You get only YOUR email sent to you and you let others do their job and make the required decisions.

NOT ENOUGH HOURS

COMMITMENT STATEMENT

I _____ do commit to do the following steps in my quest for better quality time and more of it. I will follow the guidelines outlined here to deal with such challenges. In the event that any unforeseen challenges prevent me from doing so, I will contact Owen immediately and work through a solution with him.

Date:

Signed:

The process of creating an action plan is simple. Once you are clear over what the main issues you have around time are and you have outlined your priorities and organised an effective system for yourself, you will then be in a position to decide on the main things you need to do to take charge over your time and life.

There are four elements to the plan of action:

- The Actions

- Potential Problems

- Simple Solutions

- Commitment Statement

Each one of these has its own function and reason for existing.

Decide on Actions

The plan used in *Not Enough Hours* includes four main **actions** for the participants to take and specifies when they need to take them. These four actions summarise the main things that they need to do in order to improve their time wealth and their time quality.

From the work I did with each participant in the show, I went through everything we had done, and based on their original goals and priorities, determined what the necessary actions would be.

In order to do this successfully, the key is to find out what four actions best sum up the things you need to do and to write each one of them at the top of the page. It doesn't have to be four, but the key is to limit the number, as it is better to have less to focus on, so you can do it thoroughly.

Write each main action as a one-word or two-word concept and follow that by describing in a sentence what this means you will actually do. So, you could write down the words "Switch Off" and then describe what you mean by that. For example, you could say, "Make sure that you completely free your mind from work once you leave the office."

Next, write down the time or day you will do this. Once you have done this for each of the four actions, you are ready for the next step.

Determine Potential Problems

Of course, every good plan must include the process of accounting for the obstacles that may lie ahead in terms of implementing the plan. For the people I worked with on the show, I decided to include three **potential problems** that we agreed may arise in following each of the four actions. So, in total, we outlined 12 potential pitfalls that they needed to be aware of.

We came up with those problems together, as I asked them what they thought were the most likely things that could get in their way when they took each of the actions. I also volunteered what I thought might be a challenge for them. Once we had identified these potential challenges, I placed them underneath each of the relevant actions.

So, go through each of the actions you will be taking. For each one of them, brainstorm a number of potential problems you may face in your quest of following through on those actions. Try to come up with at least three potential challenges for each action.

Develop Simple Solutions

Developing **simple solutions** was something that we again came up with together. Looking at each of the problems, the question I asked was: "If this problem occurs, then how will you solve it and get on with the actions?"

Many of the problems each person faced required solutions that we had already come up with in the show. Some challenges required the person to simply remind themselves of their priorities and why they were priorities. Some were new solutions that would allow them to handle the challenges more effectively.

You can do this by examining each of the problems and, under them, outlining the solution to them. There is always a solution to every problem. You just need to figure out what you can do that will allow you to deal successfully with those problems. There are many different solutions available to all sorts of issues throughout this book.

Design and Sign a Commitment Statement

One of the things that I was delighted with about the programme was that it made it more likely that the participants would follow the plan I set out for them. The rationale is very simple. Most people are highly motivated by how they look in front of others. The thought of appearing badly by having a problem and not following the advice given on television ensured that everyone I worked with was sufficiently motivated. But there are other ways to ensure such motivation.

For example, this motivation is compounded by the presence of the **commitment statement**. There's a law in psychology known as the "law of commitment", which states that people are much more likely to follow through on something once they have made a commitment on something.

We live in a world of contracts. When you buy something by cheque or take a new job, your signature is what makes it happen. So, with that in mind, I got each participant to sign a commitment statement saying that they would take the actions outlined in the plan of action and that, if they faced any problems, they would take the steps of the solutions we proposed. Lastly, it said that if they faced a problem that we had not mentioned, they would contact me and we would figure out a solution together.

Signing their commitment statement really forced them to take the plan of action seriously. It meant that if they followed the plan, they would get the results they were looking for, and if they didn't, then they would not. It firmly put the responsibility for results in their hands, and with the clock ticking every second, they were under pressure to rethink their time expenditure and start making more hours available for themselves.

The following is an example of the commitment statement I used in the show, but slightly changed. In the original I suggested they contact me in the event of an unforseen challenge. Unfortunately, this is not very helpful for you (although I'm always happy to hear from new friends!) but you can find a friend of yours who agrees to be there for you to talk to and help you figure out a solution. Again, you have this book, which is full to the brim with tips and ideas and the solution to any of the things you face may well be in here.

I, _____, do commit fully and completely to this plan of action, that I will perform all actions declared within to the best of my ability. In the event of any foreseen problems I will use the specified solution outlined. In the event of any unforeseen problems, I will talk with _____ (insert friend's name) about potential solutions and decide upon the best option.

Signed:_____

Date: _____

An Action Plan for this Book

You can use the template below to identify your own actions, potential problems and creative solutions. Identify three different problems you may have in implementing these actions and use the book to come up with solutions for each of them. On the following page are four examples of actions you could take related to the ideas in this book.

Action Plan Template

Action 1: Analyse Your Time	Action 2: Prioritise Your Actions	Action 3: Organise Your Life	Action 4: Implement This Plan
When:	When:	When:	When:
Where:	Where:	Where:	Where:
Potential Problem 1:	Potential Problem 1:	Potential Problem 1:	Potential Problem 1
Solution 1:	Solution 1:	Solution 1:	Solution 1:
Potential Problem 2:	Potential Problem 2:	Potential Problem 2:	Potential Problem 2:
Solution 2:	Solution 2:	Solution 2:	Solution 2:
Potential Problem 3:	Potential Problem 3:	Potential Problem 3:	Potential Problem 3:
Solution 3:	Solution 3:	Solution 3:	Solution 3:

Now you have your action plan, it is time to implement it. To help you, in the next section, I have also included plenty of tips and suggestions which might be of assistance in allowing you to save time in different areas of your life.

SECTION 7

TIME FOR YOUR LIFE

In this section, I outline the main areas related to time with which I've found most people struggle. I offer lots of different suggestions that might be useful and handy for you. Not all of these hints and ideas will be relevant and applicable to you and some will certainly seem common sense and you will already do them. However, I hope that there will be some that can help you greatly.

Some of them are designed to help you save time, while others are suggestions on how to better spend your time. What you choose to take from this section will depend on what priorities you have established and on what you choose to focus.

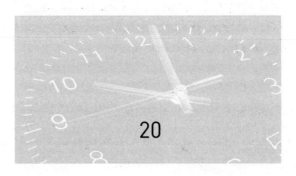

20

Time for Housework

"My second favourite household chore is ironing.
My first being hitting my head on the top bunk
bed until I faint."

ERMA BOMBECK

Housework here includes cooking, cleaning, tidying, laundry, ironing, chores, errands, messages, shopping and any jobs required on a regular basis in living your life. In this chapter, I outline some suggestions that might allow you to save time accomplishing these tasks.

First, a couple of overall points. It's useful to put daily, weekly and monthly chores in a simple schedule. Doing this will ensure that you remember to do what needs to get done. Also, put each chore through the 4D system. Do you need to do it now or later? Can you give it to someone else to do or skip doing it altogether? Remember, some chores can be done at the same time and multi-tasking is often a good idea for tasks which require little mental effort. It is also an idea to listen to CDs or watch DVDs when you are doing a menial task, as you are killing two birds with one stone.

Time to Cook

1   Have meals based around interesting themes.

2   Organise meals using similar ingredients over the course of two days' cooking.

3   Use two types of ingredients, perishable and non-perishable. Buy non-perishables in large quantities once a month.

4   Cook a few meals at once that store well.

5   Have a set place for take-out and delivery menus.

6   Set a timer to go off when it's time to start dinner. Use a portable timer that you can bring with you so you can attend to other tasks while you wait for the timer to go off.

7   Make a timeline and work backwards. Decide when you want to serve dinner and ask yourself what you have to have done by then.

8   Clean as you cook.

9   Spray the cooking and preparing food surface with non-stick spray before using it.

10 Prepare in advance and freeze all the foods that store well which you can eat later on.

11 Plan two weeks' meals in advance. Make a list of meals that you all enjoy and plan different meals.

12 Write down all the ingredients needed for the various menus.

13 Fit the menu around your lifestyle. Set easy-to-make dinners that require less time.

14 Use leftovers from dinner for lunch the following day when possible. If you have turkey, then maybe have sandwiches with the turkey left over.

15 Make cooking into a family activity or quality time with your partner. It's so much more fun when you do it with others!

Time to Clean

Nobody likes living in a dirty house. Most people will make a real effort to ensure that their house, car and living space look as well as possible. There is a difference, however, between cleaning and obsessive cleaning. Obsessive cleaning, as we saw with Marina, can be a huge drain on your time.

Here I want to explore the difference between the different types of cleaning. For example, tidying is something that can be done daily whereas cleaning is something best done weekly. I believe all cleaning can be categorised into four types:

- On-the-spot cleaning

- Tidying

- Weekly cleaning

- Intensive cleaning

On-the-Spot Cleaning

On-the-spot cleaning means cleaning something as you go. This saves a large amount of time because, for a few extra seconds, you save yourself one big cleaning effort.

1   For example, washing the dishes are best done as you go. Most people wait for all the dishes to pile up and then do a big clean. You can actually save yourself quite a bit of time by washing and drying the dishes immediately after you use them. Of course, if you have a dishwasher, you can still clean as you go by rinsing the dishes and placing them in the dishwasher immediately after use.

2   Not wearing shoes around the house will also save you a lot of unnecessary cleaning. Much of the dirt and grime that comes into a house comes from wearing shoes. Of course, shoes should be placed near the door so you have handy access to them. Slippers placed in the same area can remind you to switch into them immediately.

3   Get other members of the family into the habit of cleaning on the spot as they go. When they build it as a habit, there will be a lot less to clean.

4   Have a litter bin in each room and make sure you use them whenever you need them.

5   Hang up your clothes or put them in the laundry basket immediately after you have finished wearing them.

6 Have tissues in plentiful supply in different rooms of the house as well.

7 As soon as you get out of the bath or shower, give it a quick wipe and get rid of excess water.

8 When you use the sink, give it a quick wipe afterwards.

9 Put DVDs and CDs back in their cases when you are finished using them.

10 Make your bed after you get out of it in the morning. (Obviously wait if someone else is still sleeping there!)

Tidying

Tidying is something you can do once a day or so. It involves immediate tasks that take away some of the clutter and mess that you see when you enter a room. When you have finished tidying a room, it should look clear and clean at first glance.

1 Wipe off sticky shelves or countertops.

2 Throw out junk mail immediately.

3 Create one place for remote controls to be stored and put them there.

4 Before you go to bed, do a quick pick-up/tidy of sitting-room.

5 Keep CDs/DVDs in order.

6 Before leaving the room in the morning, clear any table or chair tops of stray items and clothing.

7 Put all items in the right place the first time.

8 Take out rubbish and recycle regularly.

9 Make sure you have the normal and recycle bins beside each other and become clear and disciplined about what goes in each bin.

10 Give the room a quick sweep to get rid of any dust or clutter.

Weekly Cleaning

Weekly cleaning is more thorough than tidying but less so than an intensive cleaning. Here, you are cleaning enough to make sure that things are looking well but stopping short of detailed dusting. At the end of a weekly clean, the room should still look clean after a more careful inspection.

The important point here is that if you have been conducting on-the-spot cleaning and tidying regularly then you won't have much cleaning to do. Here are some suggestions:

1 Make cleaning supplies easy to get to and to put away.

2 Break down cleaning into small tasks. Write down what you are going to clean.

3 Don't over-clean. Sometimes you can spend far too long on something that already looks fine.

Learn to tell the difference between something being done and overdone.

4 Set yourself a small reward for finishing the weekly cleaning.

5 Be pragmatic with magazines: unread magazines and catalogues should be thrown out or stored somewhere out of the way if you are certain you will need them one day.

6 Toss outdated food and keep fridge and freezer clean. Also ensure that all kitchen utensils are kept clean.

7 Check under beds, desks, chairs and couches for dust gathering and use a vacuum cleaner or sweeping brush to remove it entirely.

Intensive Cleaning

Intensive cleaning is a monthly or bi-monthly clean from top to bottom of the house. This will involve getting into nooks and crannies that you often miss out during a weekly clean. Of course, there is also an annual clean or spring cleaning that many people do, which is an even more extreme version of the intensive clean. However, if you ensure you keep up with the intensive clean, you may not need to do a spring clean!

1 Schedule in half a day or a full day once a month or once every two months to give the whole house a big clean.

2   Get help from the family for this big task and arrange a fun reward for everybody, including yourself, afterwards.

3   Make a list of everything you need to clean and break it down into sections.

4   Ensure that you have all the cleaning materials necessary and if you don't, get them all ready before you begin. Put them near the place that they will be used to clean.

5   Set yourself a time limit for each section and focus on getting the job done as well and as thoroughly as possible.

6   Hire a professional cleaning company for these big jobs if you feel it is something you would be comfortable with. You can always give it the once-over after they have finished, which will take you a lot less time.

7   Have a look around for anything that is out of place and keep things organised so that they are easy to find.

Time to Shop

Many people waste a lot of time shopping. Marina, for example, spent a lot of time going to and from the shops buying groceries and fresh food. During the programme, I brought Marina and her children to a cooking expert, a trainer in the "Cooks Academy". We learned from her that it is indeed possible to have fresh food and buy it all once or twice a week.

So, the key to efficient shopping is careful planning. When you are clear on exactly what you need, then you are much more likely to avoid extra trips to the shop.

1 Make a list of everything you need to buy. This list might be the same most weeks but there might be a monthly list with some extra items each month. Buy in bulk if you have a place to store things.

2 Try the internet, which is fast becoming a popular place to shop. Do your research and figure out if it would be worth it to shop on the web. Tesco Online is a good example of a resource available for online grocery shopping. It can really speed things up once you get used to it.

3 Take your list with you and avoid straying from it. Impulsive buying is often a waste of time and money. By sticking to the list, you can ensure that you will get things done in the shortest amount of time.

4 Shop late at night or early in the morning to avoid crowds. Most shops are now open longer hours. Find the time there are less crowds and you won't have to deal with long lines or big traffic queues.

5 Become familiar with the supermarket you go to and record which aisles everything is on. With a little thoughtfulness, you can ensure that you maximise the speed with which you get the shopping done by writing your list in order according to the supermarket layout.

6 Pack the groceries in the same order that you will be taking them out and keep them together in similar piles.

7 As soon as you get home, put all the groceries away. Get into this habit as it takes a couple of extra minutes but saves you time later on.

8 Whenever you are getting a new item with a specified make or model, take the old item with you to ensure that you get the right one.

9 Before any big purchase, do your research. Check which shops it is available in and check online sites as well. Ensure that you know exactly what you want and what the choices are so you can make the best one possible.

10 Before clothes shopping, make a list of what clothes you want to buy. Decide on what shops you are going to visit for these clothes and in what order.

11 Create a folder for gift cards and vouchers and when you come home place the cards together in this folder.

12 Create a folder for receipts and again when you get home, place the receipts in the folder.

13 Buy some generic birthday, wedding and newborn cards and small gifts. It ensures that you are always ready should a short notice event come up. The same is true for toys. Having some generic toys at the ready saves you time for christenings or birthday parties you or your children might be invited to.

14 Fit in other tasks to do when you go shopping. For example, on your way to the shops, visit the bank or post office if they are nearby.

Time for Appointments

We all have hair appointments, dentist appointments, doctor appointments and lots of other meetings that we arrange throughout the day. Most of the time, we will have at least a say in when these appointments are going to be. The trick is to make them fit into your schedule as effectively as possible. Here are some tips on doing this:

1 Do your best to organise appointments which are located close to each other so you can do two in a row or combine them with some other chores in the same area if you can.

2 Try to get the first appointment of the day or the first after lunch. This usually ensures that you will start on time.

3 Bring something to read or a notebook to work on when going to an appointment.

4 Call ahead and confirm. The worst waste of time is going there and finding out that you have the wrong time.

5 Be clear about the address before you set off. Another huge waste of time is going there and finding out you have the wrong address.

6   Ensure that you are on time. Often you can miss your appointment altogether if you are late for it.

7   Bring your schedule with you in case you need to arrange another appointment at the end.

Time for Laundry

Laundry is one of those time-consuming activities that can creep up on you and take valuable minutes out of your day. Here are some ideas on how you can minimise the time it takes.

1   Have a laundry basket available in your room and place clothes in it instead of on chairs, the bed or the floor.

2   Have a place especially for socks and underwear and make them easy to access.

3   Keep the same place for taking out clothes for washing and putting back laundry. Have a bag into which you can place the folded clothes before you put them in their necessary location.

4   Keep clothes that are in season or that you wear often in easy-to-reach places.

5   Use the washing machine overnight so that your laundry is washing while you are sleeping.

6   Sort laundry into different groups for different types . . . dry cleaning, whites, colours, etc.

7   Make sure you dry the clothes properly. If you do so you will have less to iron.

8   If items are left sitting in the dryer too long after the cycle has finished, then toss in a damp towel and dry again on a warm setting. This will reduce the need to iron.

9   Another way to reduce the amount of ironing is to hang up shirts, trousers, tops and dresses on a hanger in the bathroom when you take a shower. The steam from the shower will often straighten out the creases and iron them for you.

10   When you do iron, learn how to do it properly so you only need to do it once. When you have finished, carefully fold the clothes or put them straight on hangers so that you keep them crease free. Once this habit becomes automatic, you can iron while doing something else, for example, learning a new language on CD or watching the television.

11   Have a sewing box handy in case something needs to be fixed.

12   Learn to get rid of clothes. Throw out clothes which are ripped and torn (unless you can fix them to your satisfaction). Throw out clothes which are too small for you or clothes that you haven't worn in a year (unless they have genuine sentimental value, are designed for a particular activity such as painting which you haven't done in a while, or can be given to someone else, in which case you can place them in the back of the press).

Some Other General Points on Housework

1 Ensure that you have a place to put your keys so that you always remember them.

2 Put out all you need for the next day the night before and make sure you are thorough.

3 Become aware of how long different tasks take and ensure that you schedule them cleverly.

4 Say No when there is too much to do.

5 Learn to tolerate imperfection or untidiness from time to time.

6 Ensure that family quality time is non-moveable and takes precedence over housework.

7 Create a lost-and-found basket so that everyone can find things when they lose them.

8 Keep all family events on a calendar and remind everyone of when each event is happening. Plan ahead for special events. For example, prepare for Christmas as outlined below.

Time for Christmas

1 Prepare a list of everyone you need to send cards to and make sure you have their addresses.

2 Make a list of everyone you need to buy presents for. Take into account your budget for presents and what you think would suit the person. The more you decide ahead of time what to buy them, the easier it will be to shop.

3 Write down a list of everything you will need for Christmas dinner. Also compile a task list for Christmas Day. Go out and buy all the ingredients you will need for Christmas dinner.

4 List all the people you need to call or email over Christmas. Take half a day out over Christmas to make calls or send emails to people you want to stay in touch with.

5 Buy the amount of cards that you need plus a few extra. Make sure you have envelopes and stamps.

6 When buying presents, make sure you have an idea which shops you need to go to so you can blitz through the shops more effectively. You can also try to buy in as few shops as possible and use catalogues so you know whether or not the shop has what you are looking for.

7 Make sure you have some quality time for yourself. With all the responsibilities, it's essential for you to take some "me" time.

8 Enjoy the time you spend with your family. One of the main elements of Christmas is being with your loved ones. Make the times as wonderful as possible and leave work at work.

Time for Others

*"Come out of the circle of time
And into the circle of love."*

RUMI

Time for others involves quality time that you spend with other people. Whether it is time to find a partner, time to spend with your partner, time for your children or the elderly or time for socialising with your friends, time for others is about making time to spend with the people that matter in your life. This chapter is full of practical tips to free up and best use your time with others.

Time to Meet

Many people assume that being single and not having any ties to a partner or children naturally means that you have plenty of free time. Instead, there are many single people who find themselves as busy as and sometimes even busier than they would be with a family.

Being single for many is connected with freedom. The problem with freedom is that it allows you a whole list of choices that you wouldn't have available to you if you had responsibilities. All these choices mean that there are lots more tasks you can take on, and many people do so.

What this means is that there is much less time made available for things like dating and meeting people. With our busy lives, it becomes harder and harder for us to make time available for relationships.

It is essential to make time for meeting people and dating. The dating landscape has changed in Ireland and throughout the world. Here are some ways to improve your chances of meeting the right person:

1   The internet is now an acceptable and, for many, a usual way of meeting people. We spend so much time at our computers that it is a convenient way of getting to know people. Give internet dating a try. Even social networking sites like Facebook can be a great way to meet people, but remember that such distance relationships can take away precious time from real face-to-face friendships and potential partners.

2   If you are looking for love, you need to be open to any possible opportunities. Join any clubs or societies where you might get to meet like-minded people.

3   Chat to more people and become more sociable in all sorts of situations. Start a conversation with people on the train or bus. Say hello to people when you are

at the bar. There are all sorts of opportunities to meet people.

4 Smile more. It makes you look a lot more approachable to others.

5 Give special events like speed-dating a go.

6 Take time to look your best whenever you go out. Be a catch at all times.

7 Learn to like yourself more. The more you like yourself, the easier it is for others to like you.

8 Laugh more. The more of a laugh you have with another person, the more they will want to spend time with you.

9 Make them feel good about themselves when they are with you. The better you make another person feel, the more they will want to spend time with you.

10 Be independent and happy in your own company. This is far more attractive than fawning all over others.

11 Be creative with the dates you go on. Find new ways to have fun with them.

12 Pay attention to the other person and remember the things that matter to them.

Time for Romance

John was 37 and had been married for five years. His wife, Sarah, supported him throughout his career as a busy journalist. At 35, three years after they got married, he took a job down the country, as it paid far better than anything else he had. Soon, John was gone five days out of seven, with the constant excuse that he was doing it to provide the best life for both of them. To his wife, the best life involved having John beside her. She could not survive in this situation. So, finally, she moved out after plenty of warnings, which John never took seriously.

The truth is that we often take our relationships for granted. We live under the illusion that they will definitely always be there. We especially take our loved ones for granted, and assume that because they are understanding we can let them down more than others.

Richard Bandler pointed out to me once that we often take out our bad feelings on the ones we love the most while we treat complete strangers with kindness and courtesy. This makes no sense whatsoever. Now, I'm not suggesting taking bad feelings out on strangers, although that would be fun! What it is about is appreciating the love of your life and making a conscious effort to be nicer to them.

If you have found someone you are with in a happy relationship, then you are one of the lucky ones. It's essential to appreciate that and enjoy the fact.

When you are in a relationship, there are certain tips that might help you make the most of things:

1 It's important that you work on it and make sure you place your attention on improving it. Because we often take our relationships for granted, it is easy to get stuck in a rut where we become so absorbed with our busy lives that we forget to appreciate what we have. Meeting someone that we

really love and who feels the same for us is extremely fortunate.

2   We often discuss time with each other as "luxury time". It is vital that you make sure that this luxury time becomes necessity time.

3   It's amazing how many long-term couples I meet who make very little time together. Often the time they spend together is their joint housework or looking after the children. Make your priority of the love of your life a reality. Create quality time for each other.

4   Organise regular dates with your partner. Either go out somewhere special or stay in and have dinner and watch a movie or do something fun together; the key is to ensure that you make the environment as special and as romantic as possible. Recreate the atmosphere of your earliest dates.

5   Reminisce with your partner about the fun times. Chat about how you met, your feelings then, and relive the excitement, the delight and fun that you had together back then. It really helps to make you feel even more grateful for having each other.

6   Remember important dates in your diary such as birthdays and anniversaries. Failure to do so will have devastating consequences.

7   Buy thoughtful and romantic gifts for your partner and surprise them from time to time with a well-thought-out gift or experience.

Time to Make Love

It would be ludicrous to put making love or sex on your "to-do" list, yet it is a good idea to plan that it *will* happen. One of the things that makes the experience so wonderful is its spontaneity. It feels as if both partners are overcome by their lust and love for each other, which is a romantic notion. But you can still plan for it and make it *feel* just as spontaneous.

The secret is to plan a very romantic time with each other. Create the right conditions and make it as appealing for both of you as possible. You don't need to mention sex, but make sure you have a flirtatious smile on your face when you plan the special evening. A special wink and nudge can increase the excitement.

Make sure you set things up so that you get your partner in the mood. Remember what kinds of things turn your partner on and make the experience as exciting as possible. This will also help rekindle the romantic spark between you, even after years, if it needs a little reigniting.

The most important thing to do is to ensure that you both lose yourselves in the experience. Allow yourself to just enjoy feeling pleasure and helping your partner feel as much pleasure as possible also. It needs to be something that you can let go into fully and avoid thinking about your daily routines.

It can be easy to slip into nightly habits such as reading or watching TV, which can kill the mood. Instead, prioritise intimate time by including sensual pleasures such as a long, warm bath or a soothing massage.

Of course, the spontaneous quickie and the long, passionate love-making session both have their upside and downside and can be enjoyed whenever the time is right. But making love is something to make time for, as it is one of the most enjoyable and connecting experiences you can have with your partner.

Time for the Family

It is also crucial that you set aside some time for the rest of your family and friends. I am not talking about just doing things *for* them. Of course, you help each other out, but what I mean is taking some quality time on a regular basis to spend with the people in your life who are close to you and who enjoy each other's company. Here are some things to remember:

1   In each of your relationships, ask how you would want the other person to think of you. Start acting like this.

2   Make sure you remember important occasions such as birthdays.

3   Schedule in some quality, fun time with your family.

4   Avoid taking out your problems on your loved ones.

5   Find fun activities that you can all do together.

6   Arrange regular visits to different members of the family and make sure they are available when you call.

Time for the Elderly

Eventually we will all run out of time. For the final years of our life, some of us are left lonely and alone. For some, we might not be alone but we might still feel lonely.

My granny has suffered from dementia for a number of years. She does not remember very much and is sometimes confused but she still remembers that I am someone familiar. I don't know what it's like to be elderly and I have no idea what it is like to be my granny. But I do know that visiting my granny makes a difference to her. She just doesn't want to be alone and spending time with her is the best gift anyone can give to her.

So often in this world, we find ourselves so caught up in our busy lives that we don't have time to visit our elderly relatives. "They won't notice," we think. "Sure, we don't really do anything when we get there, anyway." But time spent with them makes a huge difference. For once, *any* time is quality time, because they need someone to be there for them, with them. I think it's extremely important to be there for the elderly.

Time for Children

One of the most common phrases I have heard from the participants in the programme, as well as from many of my own friends and colleagues, is the old adage: "Having children completely changes your life." Each week as I visited each person and I got to share in their lives, I realised how true it was.

When you have children, nothing is ever the same again and a large proportion of your time is delegated to them. Your concept of time changes and you have less space and fewer hours than ever. You do your very best to avoid having your child end up as a "latchkey child" who spends their time alone most of the time. Instead, you want to be there for them, but having many other responsibilities makes this harder.

Below are some tips for best using your time with babies, as well as having fun with, educating and organising older children.

Time for Babies

When babies first come along and we try to grapple with being a parent, we are forced to completely switch around our schedules and to deal with much more responsibility. Babies need constant care. Here are some suggestions which might help you:

1   Give yourself some time alone with your baby after their birth to get used to each other before taking visitors. Make sure your friends know not to visit until you have settled into your new routine.

2   Build a regular routine for babies which they can get used to so it's easier to get them to sleep in the evening.

3   Develop some flexibility in the routine and don't be afraid to vary from it if necessary.

4   Write a list of every name and number a babysitter will need in looking after your baby.

5 Write out detailed instructions on everything for your babysitter.

6 For bath times, keep a basket in the bathroom with all the necessary items in it.

7 Keep nappies and baby stuff in a bag in the car.

Time for Fun

Doing housework while children watch the TV is not quality time. Taking the children shopping is not quality time. This is multi-tasking so that you can do the things that need to be done while keeping the kids occupied.

Of course, we find ourselves trying to be the perfect parents and in so doing, we try to take care of all of the housework. Our children must live in a clean and tidy house. They must be well fed and groomed and they must get to school and any after-school activity they want to go to. Most parents feel this way and this is okay. The problem comes when all of that is at the expense of quality time.

Quality time here means spending time with the children that you all enjoy and have fun. It's time for time's sake and does not include trying to achieve some material goal during the process. It's about emotional nourishment as well as physical nourishment. Here are some examples of quality time:

1 Play with them. Children play and love playing. It's how they learn about the world, people and themselves and it allows them to use their

imaginations creatively. When playing with them, let yourself return to the mindset of a child. It is so much fun playing with babies and young children, as long as you let yourself go and enjoy the process. This means using your imagination the same way they do. If you are concerned about the tidy-up afterwards, confine the play to a particular room, but let yourself go wild in that room. Research shows that play is one of the single greatest contributions to a child's self-esteem and learning potential.

2 Bedtime stories are another wonderful way of spending quality time with your children. When reading to children, put on the voices of the different characters. This helps the child really relate to the story and it's lots of fun as well. Even if your voice is awful, you will get them laughing anyway!

3 Go to the zoo. Anybody who goes to the zoo knows that there are lots of children there and for good reason. Children tend to love animals, so bringing them to the zoo is a terrific way to spend a few hours every few weeks. It's very educational, thoroughly enjoyable and they get fresh air and exercise at the same time.

4 Do fun activities. From bowling to the cinema to snooker to crazy golf, there are lots of different activities you can do with children that they will enjoy and will challenge them and help them have a good time with you. The key is always to participate yourself and get into the spirit of the things.

5 Get out of the house. As well as the obvious benefits to our health of going outside, bringing the children away from what they are used to ensures that they become more familiar with the world. This makes the time spent more valuable, as they are experiencing the world around them and getting used to it. Also, it means that you have less mess to waste time cleaning up as well!

Time for Educating

As well as emotional nourishment, it is also a good thing to focus on intellectual nourishment. You should spend a reasonable amount of time helping your children develop and improve.

1 Buy children lots of creative and interactive toys. Encourage them to let their imaginations run wild and have fun exploring their ideas. Introduce them to educational toys and books as well. Help them to get into the habit of enjoying learning about things.

2 Find out what desirable role models they have and learn about them. You might be able to motivate your children to learn more by showing them how their role model has improved themselves. When they discover that their favourite footballer or pop star can speak two languages, it may encourage them to learn languages.

3 When they are curious, encourage them to find out for themselves and help them sometimes. Be patient with them and praise them once they have found out.

4   Always praise them for anything they have accomplished successfully. They need to learn from an early age that it's good to give things a go.

5   Help them figure out how to improve. Always ask them what they think they could improve and help them train themselves to see things in a different and more useful way so that they can improve without others telling them how.

6   Encourage their creativity. Whatever games you play with them, let their minds be as open and creative as possible.

Time for Organising Children

1   Write due dates into the calendar for children's projects and essays as well as their friends' birthdays.

2   Put all borrowed books and items in the same place and be aware of when they need to go back to the library.

3   Put hospital and emergency numbers on paper near the phone.

4   Let your child be your special helper with housework one day every week.

5   Scan the calendar at the start of the week to be ready for events.

6   Create a playroom or a play space where they can mess freely and confine the messing to that space

339

so that you have a limited amount of cleaning and tidying to do.

7   Take part in car-pooling. Work with other parents to share lifts.

8   Put away toys that haven't been used in a couple of months and remember where you put them.

9   When giving instructions to a child, make sure you have their full attention to minimise the chances of you having to repeat them. (This is often a good idea to do with some adults as well.)

10 Try to schedule appointments so that you get your children taken care of at the same time e.g. hair or dental appointments back to back.

11 Do a photo collage of how time passes for your family. If you have children, it is a great idea to assemble a collection of photos of them as they grow up from the time they were born. It gets you to realise just how quickly time passes and emphasises how important every moment is.

12 Be a good example for your child in terms of how you spend your time. Demonstrate organisation, act on your priorities and develop good habits of time management and you will lead your children by example.

22

Time for Work

*"In order that people may be happy in their work,
these three things are needed: They must be fit for it.
They must not do too much of it. And they must
have a sense of success in it."*

JOHN RUSKIN

As well as the needs of our children, we must also take care of our own needs. One of these is the need to be productive, to do something. When we work, it helps us to feel like we are contributing to society in some way. Even if that contribution isn't important to us, knowing that we are earning money is. In many ways, when we work, we are doing something for our family. We are ensuring they have all the material possessions that they need.

In this chapter, I outline lots of suggestions for working at the office and at home, more efficient meetings, effectively working best with emails, the web, computers and study.

Working Tips

We are living in a far more flexible work environment than ever before. Many of us find ourselves working from home. Regardless of whether you work from your bedroom or the office in the city, here are plenty of suggestions for saving time and making the most of your time at work:

1 Make the first hour count. Get something tangible done for the first hour in the morning. Do nothing else until you get this done. That starts your day on a productive note.

2 Take regular breaks and get fresh air. Work with your own body's rhythms, take breaks when you need to and ensure that you are working at your best.

3 Associate your workplace only with work and when you take breaks step away from your desk.

4 When doing projects, ensure that the project is on the right track before working on it and getting it finished.

5 Only answer your phone during certain defined periods you set for yourself.

6 Notice the times you work best and do the most challenging elements at those times.

7 Make sure you have a tidy workspace and computer desk.

8 Put up a "do not disturb" sign for the times you don't want to be disturbed.

9 Establish your matrix of what is important and urgent and aim to focus on what is important.

10 Whenever something arrives in your in-tray, decide to do it or delegate it or defer it or delete it. If you decide to defer it, is there any of it you can do immediately?

11 Write a list of tasks "to do" tomorrow at the end of each day and include things to remember.

12 Make a list of all people you need to talk to and subjects you need to talk about.

13 Keep an eye on the calendar each day and check in to see how you are progressing on all tasks and levels.

14 Find out how much time you allocate to each action and add 20 per cent.

15 Position yourself so that you are not facing directly to the door. That way there is less chance of eye contact with someone passing by who might step in for a chat and interrupt you.

16 Keep up to date with things as you go. Answer your emails daily or every two days. Avoid having a huge backlog of emails to get back to.

17 Organise meetings close to or where you work to avoid wasting time in traffic.

18 Ensure you look after your posture and how you work to maximise productivity in the most healthy way.

19 Set up effective lighting in your office, using natural light as often as possible.

20 When people come in, stand up when talking to them. It ensures they won't stay for too long.

Time for Efficient Meetings

1 Be clear about what you want to get out of the meetings. What is to be discussed and decided upon?

2 Invite only the people to the meeting who are needed for what is being discussed.

3 Have someone describe what topics are being covered and what decisions are made and who has agreed to what action by the end of the meeting.

4 Reduce the length of time of the meeting. Define how long you will spend on each topic and make sure you have reached these answers before the time allotted ends.

5 Ensure that you have commitments from each participant in the meeting as to what they are going to do and when they are going to do it, make note of this and be prepared to follow them up on this as necessary.

6 Check with everyone in the meeting that they agree with your understanding of the decisions made and commitments promised.

7 If someone suggests something irrelevant but important, then simply note it down and suggest that you can get back to it once you have satisfactorily finished the topic you are on.

8 Keep focused on behaviours that are to be done and not on blaming people.

9 Ask reluctant contributors open-ended questions to which they can't say "yes" or "no" and encourage expanded answers.

10 Ask those who talk a lot, targeted, focused questions to keep their points relevant and concise. Keep social talk in the meeting to a minimum.

Time for Email

1 Check your email in batches twice a day unless absolutely necessary to do it once or twice more.

2 Give yourself a certain amount of time to answer emails.

3 Create folders for different people, subjects or issues, depending on what works best for you.

4 When dealing with an email, immediately file it in the relevant folder and keep your inbox as clear as possible.

5 Title all your outgoing email messages with a summary of what the email is about. This will ensure that it's easy for you to file them and find them.

6 Learn how to use your email account. There may be some features you don't know about that can help you save time.

7 Use signatures in your email with all your necessary information to avoid having to repeatedly write out this information.

8 Only email when necessary.

9 Use your autoresponder if you are away so that you can let people know you will respond to them upon your return.

10 Some people are far better to email than call. Email those people for whom email is a quicker option. Call those who are better to call.

Time for the Web

1 Mark any web pages or websites you use regularly as your Favourites or Bookmarks.

2 Mark the site you use most often as your homepage.

3 Search using + or – as well as quotes. Use + when you want to combine a search for NLP and Time Management, for example – "NLP" + "Time Management". Use – when you want to search for

NLP and *not* Time Management: "NLP" – "Time Management".

4   Identify exactly what information you are looking for and stick to finding that information.

5   Avoid all websites that waste your time. You know which ones they are!

6   Keep your computer up to date and ensure that it is protected from all spam, viruses, trojans, adware and spyware. They can all slow down your system quite significantly.

7   Get a high-speed broadband connection. It will save you an invaluable amount of time and avoid you becoming excessively frustrated.

8   Set a time limit for how long you will browse the net. Stick to it.

Time for the Computer

1   Invest in a decent and reasonably fast computer. What you might spend in money you will recoup in time saved.

2   Have detailed names for your documents for easy filing and finding.

3   Learn tricks and shortcuts on your word processor.

4   Find ways to secure and organise the cables effectively.

5 Invest time to learn to use the software before attempting to use it. The more you know, the quicker you will be in using it and the more you will get out of it.

6 If you need to switch off when you leave the office, leave your laptop there.

Time for the Phone

1 Stop giving your mobile number out to people. Only give it to those you want or need a call from.

2 Learn the features of the phone so you can use it easily.

3 Programme in your friends and frequently dialled numbers as shortcuts.

4 Use your alarm on the phone as a reminder of things you have to do.

5 Have a pad and pen beside the phone to take notes.

6 Screen your calls and decide which ones to take.

7 Find out the best time to call people back.

8 Before you call, ask yourself: "What do I want from the call?"

9 Some people are better to phone than to email. If it is quicker to call them, then do that.

10 Texting can sometimes be quicker and sometimes slower than a call. Text them if you can get away

with one or two texts. If it is a choice between a long text exchange and a conversation, choose the conversation and get to the point quickly.

Time to Study

Here are some tips on making the best use of your time when you are studying.

1 Study often. Get into a habit of reviewing what you are learning on a regular basis so it's fresh in your mind when you need to study it.

2 When completing essays and projects, review what you have learned and the main points before you move on.

3 Learn as much as you can about the exams and get as many past papers as possible.

4 Practise completing past papers in the same amount of time that you will get in the exam.

5 Study under conditions similar to exam conditions.

6 Use Mind Maps and other memory skills to improve how well you recall the material.

7 When studying, ask yourself the questions:

- What do I need to remember?

- What possible questions may I be asked?

- How can I best answer such questions?

23

Time for Yourself

"Is life not a hundred times too short for us to stifle ourselves?"

FRIEDRICH NIETZSCHE

Last, but certainly not least, is the importance of having time for yourself. Having time for yourself means ensuring that you make time for having fun, improving yourself, being healthy and happy, with friends as well as contributing to the world.

Time to Have Fun

One of the things many people don't do enough of is ensuring that they make plenty of time for themselves to have fun. This doesn't have to mean just going out drinking, as it often can in this culture. Instead, it is about finding lots of ways to enjoy your life even more and having more things to look forward to. Here are some ideas:

1   Make time for some sort of sport or hobby that involves exercise.

2   Write out a list of things you have done which you found fun.

3   Write out a list of things you have not done but would like to do because they seem fun.

4   Schedule in time to do fun things with your friends – both things you have done before and haven't yet done.

5   Make sure plenty of the fun things you do are outdoor activities.

6   Keep your TV-watching moderate, as outlined below.

Time for TV

1   Watch only the programmes that you really want to and set yourself a maximum number of hours per week.

2   Keep the remote controls in the same place and label them.

3   Avoid wasting time continuously flicking through the channels.

4   Ensure you always find programmes that will make you feel good or that you will learn from. (Of course, *Not Enough Hours* is one such programme!)

5 Invest in Sky+ or a digital recorder. This will allow you to record programmes to watch them in your own time.

Time for Photos

Learn how to use the different functions on your camera. It will actually save you time if you learn how to use it first.

1 Keep the warranty, receipts and information in a safe place.

2 Organise photos as you go either digitally or manually. Keep only the good or important ones.

3 Develop a habit of uploading digital photos immediately when you get home.

4 Buy different albums, divided and organised by date.

Time for Holidays

1 Do your research. Find out what the weather is going to be like where you are going and what kind of activities you will most likely be doing.

2 Based on this, establish what you need to buy for your trip, make a shopping list and buy them.

3 Write a list of everything you need to bring with you. Include clothes, accessories, adapters, toiletries and anything else you might need.

NOT ENOUGH HOURS

4 Pack your bags a day or two in advance. Fold your clothes as thinly as possible. Only pack what you need. Ensure that your suitcase is sturdy and strong.

5 Book your flights well in advance, check in online if possible and ensure that your suitcases are within the required weight limit.

6 Pre-book your taxi if possible for when you arrive so you don't waste time trying to track one upon arrival.

7 Before you leave the house, remove any metal objects from yourself and have them in your jacket. Make it as easy as possible for you as you go through security.

8 Ensure that you have your passport, money and tickets with you.

9 Bring a book, iPod or laptop with you for your journey.

10 Follow the guidelines on jetlag if necessary.

11 When you arrive, unpack immediately and prepare clothes for the next day.

Time to Improve

In this world of information, we have so much that we can learn it could be overwhelming. But that doesn't mean we shouldn't learn. It does mean that we should

353

make intelligent decisions about what we want to learn and how to best use our time. Here are some ideas:

1 **Learning Skills:** Learning a new skill is always a good idea. The key is to get lots of practice very regularly in order to become good at whatever you decide to learn. If you are learning to swim or to drive, for example, get plenty of lessons in a short space of time and keep disciplined attendance. That will ensure that you master the basics quickly. Then it is also important that you regularly practise it over the next few months.

2 **Reading:** Reading is something which can help you tremendously as well. Find books and subjects that interest you and do your research. What do you want to know? What do you want to learn? What books are available on this topic? Then check out bookshops and libraries, browse through different books and look at Amazon reviews of the books. The headings and chapter titles of a book should let you know if it is of interest to you and the reviews should also help you make up your mind.

3 **Doing Courses:** There are plenty of courses out there, from courses on how you can be happier and improve yourself to courses in learning a new language. The best kinds of courses are often the intensive ones, as they ensure that you are fully immersed in the entire experience and therefore are more likely to pick things up. It is obviously

better to learn a foreign language in the country that speaks that language. When that is not possible or you are doing evening classes, ensure that you take even a few minutes every night to review what you covered that week and build on your vocabulary every day.

4 **Listening to an Audio Course:** Audio courses and audio books are a great way to learn as you are usually doing something else at the same time. It is often necessary to listen to them a couple of times to become properly familiar with the information as your concentration might not always be at a peak, but nevertheless it is still a very useful and time-saving way of learning.

Time to be Healthy

Our health is one of the important issues we face. If you are healthy, you are more likely to live longer and therefore it is probably one of the biggest keys to having more time overall in your life. Health is, however, something that requires an investment of time. There are a million different systems of eating or exercising healthily out there. The key is to discover what works for you and what makes you feel healthy. The areas of health to focus on are good exercise, healthy eating and beating stress.

Here are some tips on becoming healthy:

Good Exercise

1 Exercise regularly for an hour or more at least three or four times a week.

2   Find out what kind of exercise suits you; e.g. going to the gym, playing football, power walks or runs, pilates, yoga or spinning.

3   Vary your exercise regime so that your body doesn't just acclimatise and get used to the form of exercise. Variety ensures that you get maximum benefit.

4   Ensure you partake in some activities that affect both your aerobic and anaerobic systems (constant activities that last a long time and aren't too intense, like jogging or walking, as well as short-spurt activities which are intense, such as sprinting).

5   If going to the gym, prepare a gym bag and have three different sets of gym gear so that it is easy to pack and unpack in a few moments. Keep your gym tag in this bag along with anything else you might need.

6   Schedule in exercise and when it is a priority, place it somewhere and refuse to move it.

7   To compound how important it is, arrange to meet people where you are exercising or hire a personal trainer so that either way you are expected to be there and have more motivation to exercise.

8   Keep exercise as a habit as it needs to be kept up constantly.

9   Bring an iPod when you are walking, running or going to the gym. Either let yourself relax with

your favourite music, watch the time fly by as you listen to an audio book or start learning something (a language for example).

Healthy Eating

1   Write out a list of the foods you eat which are good for you and those that are not.

2   Suggest any other foods you might like that are good for you.

3   When you go shopping ensure that your list has more items that are good for you and fewer of those that are not.

4   Have plenty of bottles of water around. Drinking water is good for you.

5   Fruit and vegetables often save you time as well as being good for you, as they are mostly easy to prepare and eat.

6   Multi-vitamins and mineral supplements are often a good way of helping with healthy eating.

7   Eat regular meals. It is often also better to eat more times a day and eat less rather than consuming big meals.

8   Take some time every once in a while to really relax over dinner. We can learn from the Slow Food Movement, which began in Italy, and from the cultures of the southern Europeans, to take time and savour the experience of a meal.

Beating Stress

Stress is a problem that can result in many other illnesses. We need to beat stress by learning how to relax and treat ourselves better. Here are some suggestions:

1 Take some time regularly to treat your body really well. Get a massage regularly enough and get your body accustomed to relaxation.

2 A visit to a spa once or twice a year can do you a world of good.

3 Take some time where you turn off all phones and computers and give yourself freedom from all contact and problems.

4 Get used to becoming mindful and staying in the present. When you stay in the present, there are no problems as problems usually come from how we think of the past or the future. Being mindful means noticing what is around you.

5 Learn to meditate or use self-hypnosis to bring yourself into a deeply relaxed state, which is beneficial for you and your brain. A very useful way of doing this is through Brian Colbert's "Tbreak" guided visualisation/trance which provides you with a comfortable state of relaxation and helps you recharge your batteries in just 13 minutes (www.nlp.ie).

6 From time to time when your concentration wanders, allow yourself to indulge in daydreaming

and let your mind escape the confines of reality for a while.

7   Do the things which you enjoy doing and schedule them into your routine regularly enough so you have them to look forward to and you have plenty of down time.

8   Find time to get out and experience nature every once in a while. Whether it is the ocean, the mountains or a forest, nature seems to have a very calming effect on most people as it is far removed from the normal hustle and bustle of the modern world.

9   Create a worry book where you write down your worries. This gets them out of your head and onto paper, which allows you clearer head space.

10   Write out a "to-do" list at the end of each evening so that you can fully leave work where it is and completely enjoy your personal life.

11   Learn to say No when you have too much on already. There are lots of ways you can do this listed in this book.

12   Organise your life better. Again, you will have learned this in earlier sections of the book. Use the ideas for sleeping better outlined earlier.

Time to be Happy

Another indicator of longevity is how happy a person is. Happy people tend to live longer than people who are miserable. Here are some ways of taking time to become happier:

1   From time to time, look at all you have to feel grateful about and enjoy being thankful for everything you have and everyone in your life.

2   Learn the tools of NLP (Neuro-Linguistic Programming) or other such courses, which is an attitude and set of skills that helps people improve the way they think, feel and communicate.

3   Treat yourself generously. Be good to yourself by talking to yourself in a kinder way, buying yourself presents from time to time and complimenting yourself more.

4   When you look at yourself in the mirror, get used to smiling at yourself brightly. It breaks any negative pattern of thinking you might have been using and gets you to feel better in that moment.

5   Go back through your life and identify four achievements you are proud of and vividly recollect them.

6   Explore any goals that you have designed and vividly imagine achieving those goals and having the kind of life you desire. Reward yourself for every step you take towards that life.

7   Challenge yourself with the kinds of activities you enjoy to enter the "flow" state.

8   Start watching fewer soaps and less news and watch more comedies. Go to comedy shows and get yourself used to laughing a lot more. Seriousness is one of the worst problems we face in the world and laughter is the cure. Take more time to laugh more.

9   When you meet a mood Hoover (someone who sucks out good feelings in a room through their negativity), stay away from them or make it your mission to feel good around them regardless.

10 Put the ideas of this book into practice. If you don't, it's just another waste of time!

Time for your Friends

We have never been so isolated as we are today. Although we have more and more ways of keeping in touch with people, we still seem far removed from them. We have friends all over the world but rarely get to see them. Friends are among the first things to get dropped when other priorities, such as work, take over.

Here are some good ways to keep close with your friends:

1   Find out when all your friends' birthdays are and make sure you have a way of tracking them. Send them a birthday card or e-card or at the very least a phone call or text.

2   Get your friends' addresses and send them Christmas cards every year to let them know they are in your thoughts.

3   Make an effort every three or four months to contact friends whom you haven't spoken to in ages.

4   Make an effort every couple of years to visit friends who live in other countries.

5   Organise a night out at least once a month that you spend with your friends who live close to home. Make this a priority and do something fun which lets you catch up at the same time.

6   Go to concerts, sports events, plays, movies, comedy shows or whatever else you find fun.

7   Take your closest friends along with you when you go clothes shopping and take them for lunch in return for their help. You get to spend quality time chatting with them and help with your style at the same time.

Time to Contribute

Contribution makes the world such a great place to be. Since we all live together in the world, taking time to contribute to each other's world is a valuable use of time. Here are some ideas on volunteering your time:

1   Take time out to volunteer in local sports or youth clubs in your community.

2   Volunteer in your church community or diocese.

3   Do some work in a nursing home or special needs centre.

4 Take some time out to work with the needy in a developing country.

5 Keep your environment clean and use recycling bags.

6 Find creative ways to help the environment.

7 Give your seat on the bus up for someone who needs it more.

8 Help someone who is in need of help.

24

Conclusion
Having the Time of Your Life

"Happiness depends upon ourselves."

ARISTOTLE

Some of this book was written while the 2008 American presidential campaign was in its final stages. As I heard the candidates speak, I was fascinated by their powerful rhetorical promises to change things. The American reputation abroad had been damaged badly and their economy was in a mess. As I listened to the various promises and speeches in the closing days, I heard them promising that they would make a difference. But this difference, they insisted, was something that every American voter could participate in by using their ballot.

The power of one person to change things has always fascinated me. Since I was very young, I have always been interested in extremely charismatic and inspirational leaders who could persuade large groups to transform things. I was intrigued by the process of getting people to take action. As I wrote this book, I wondered to myself: How could I convince you to take action? How could I convince you to use what you have read here?

The ideas I have outlined in this book work. It's that simple. If you take them and employ them in your life, you will find yourself having more time and spending that time in more valuable ways. The real questions are: Will you employ them? Will you take these ideas and use them? Will you take responsibility for your life and make the changes necessary to make a real difference?

You see, I believe our failure to manage our life and our failure to manage our time are very important topics. The media declare the financial crisis to be a gigantic problem that we all face. Maybe it is, but meanwhile, as we find ourselves floundering with stress at the prospect of not having enough money, we simultaneously resign ourselves to a life where we are consistently out of time. This resignation is unnecessary.

Whereas to change the financial situation of the world we need to hope our leaders can make the right decisions, the wonderful news is that we can turn around the time crisis by making changes in our own lives. We can be our own leaders and we can implement our own policies on the hours that we have at our disposal. Furthermore, by doing so, we allow ourselves to do the very best we can with our lives, regardless of what economic climate is waiting in the outside world.

Of course, the time culture is something we have to respect and understand. Depending on where we come from and our own culture, we have a variety of different ways in which we think about time. The evolution of timekeeping, invention of clocks and the industrial revolution have pressed us into a situation where time is no longer a subjective choice but an objective ruler.

Modern technology and the advancement of opportunities throughout the world have speeded everything up and we have come face-to-face with a world where there is far too much to do and far too little time to do it. But we can do something about this. We can take our 24 hours and by a simple change in focus learn to see time from a new perspective.

We can listen to our body clock, understand it and work with it to maximise how well, energised and healthy we are. We can develop a more useful attitude towards time and learn to think about time in new ways. We can discover our own ability to make the great moments seem to last long and the challenges to fly by. We can begin the process of using language in new ways that help us set ourselves free from the restrictions we impose on ourselves through our limited modes of thinking.

When we make these changes, we are choosing to take charge of our own lives, our own destinies. When we analyse our life and where we spend our time; when we investigate what kind of time tendencies we have; and when we allow ourselves to spot those factors which rob us of time, we can begin to take control over how we spend every moment.

We can learn to prioritise and find out what is most important to us and ensure that we keep those priorities and make them realities. We can start to create goals for ourselves to move towards and start to build the kind of life that we want. We can organise, plan and prepare ourselves to use our hours in the best way we can. We can make these plans real by developing new habits that we keep. These new habits are habitual ways of thinking, feeling and behaving which will allow us to start having the time of our lives.

One day, I will be dying and if I get a chance to look back on my life from my deathbed, I want to look back with no regrets. I want to look back and smile gratefully for the decisions I have made. I want to feel proud of the way I have spent my time on the planet.

Far too many times at funerals, I have heard people utter the immortal words, "It just shows you what truly matters in life". They declare their intent to spend more time with their families and create more balance in their lives. But then, after two weeks, with all the best intentions in the world, they go back to the way they were. They forget the lesson of the fleeting nature of life.

That is a lesson of which we must always remind ourselves. We must learn from it every day in order to ensure that we give the example to ourselves and our loved ones that we will see our lives for what they are. The programme *Not Enough Hours* is really about getting people to examine their lives, to see where their lives are going. Most people, when they see this, realise that they get the chance to make a decision that can change their world. Through this book, I hope you can make a similar decision.

This book is written to convince you that you can make a real difference to your life. It is written to convince you that learning to use your time better makes a crucial difference in your life. It is written to offer you a set of tools, ideas and a system to help you to do just this.

For all the mothers who have no time for themselves, for all the fathers who need to make more time for their children, for all those who have too much to do and too little time to do it, the question is very simple. What will you do? Will you take charge over your own destiny and decide to be responsible for taking over your time?

It's easy to shy away and complain and argue that we can't be helped. It's easy to make excuses and criticise. But it can also be easy to turn around and decide, once and for all, that we will make every single moment of our lives count, that we will make our lives special.

We have many more decisions to make than we have ever had. We have many more things we can do than we have ever had. We have many more years that we will be alive than we have ever had. In our world of so much time and so much opportunity, we need to learn to make better decisions and plan things more effectively.

When we do, we will live in a world where we have just enough hours to do the things that we want to do. We will live in a world where we will be able to enjoy the moments of our lives. We will live in a world where we will be able to look back at our lives, with no regrets and a grateful smile and sense of pride. Proud that we made the most of the years we had on this planet.

There is so much we can do and although we can't do it all, we can do some wonderful things. We can spend more afternoons playing with our children. We can find ourselves being more organised and punctual and being there on time for the important events that make a difference. Through a little analysis, prioritising and organising, we can create a positive, brilliant future out of our own chaotic worlds. We can start having the time of our life by creating time for our life.

Whether it is in learning to enjoy the moment or finding ways to become more efficient and effective; whether it is in developing the ability to say No or the insight to take some quality time for ourselves; whether it is in our planning for our future or our determination to save more time; regardless, when we realise we have a choice to take control over the time we have and when we remember that the time of our life is the most valuable quality we have, then we can choose to live a far happier and more wonderful existence.

We only get one chance at our life. We need to make it count. And we need to remember the following: We might not be Santa Claus, but we are still capable of a lot more than we ever thought possible.

RECOMMENDED RESOURCES

Here are some books and products available if you are interested
in improving the quality of your life.

Books on Time and Time Management:

Give Me Time by The Mind Gym

Getting Things Done by Dave Allen

Do it Tomorrow by Mark Forster

The Seven Habits of Highly Effective People by Steven Covey

The Time Trap by R. Alec Mackenzie

1000 Quick and Easy Time Saving Strategies by Jamie Novak

Other Recommended Books:

Conversations with Richard Bandler by Richard Bandler and
Owen Fitzpatrick

Get the Life You Want by Richard Bandler
(edited by Owen Fitzpatrick)

Richard Bandler's Guide to Trance-formation by Richard Bandler
(edited by Garner Thompson)

Persuasion Engineering by Richard Bandler and John LaValle

Time for a Change by Richard Bandler

The Charisma Code by Owen Fitzpatrick *(forthcoming)*

Quantum Psychology by Robert Anton Wilson

Change your Life in Seven Days by Paul McKenna

Tony Buzan's books are available through
www.buzanbooks.com

Audio/Video Products:

Rest of Your Life CD by Brian Colbert
(www.nlp.ie)

T-Break CD Brian Colbert
(www.nlp.ie)

Lovin' your Life CD by Owen Fitzpatrick
(www.nlp.ie)

Happy Daze DVD set by Brian Colbert
(www.nlp.ie)

Adventures in Charisma DVD set by Owen Fitzpatrick
(www.nlp.ie)

Recommended Websites:

For more information on training courses with Owen Fitzpatrick and Brian Colbert of the Irish Institute of NLP, check out www.nlp.ie, where you will learn about Life Enhancement, NLP Practitioner, NLP Business Practitioner, NLP Master Practitioner and Life and Business Coaching courses.

Also check out www.owenfitzpatrick.com for trainings with Owen on NLP, Life Management and Charisma. Owen also does corporate coaching and training.

For more information on *Not Enough Hours* check out www.rte.ie/notenoughhours

Irish Institute of NLP

Featuring the ONLY TWO LICENSED
NLP MASTER TRAINERS IN IRELAND

Owen Fitzpatrick and Brian Colbert co-founded the Irish Institute of NLP (Neuro-Linguistic Programming) in 2001. Brian Colbert, known for his work as the Mind Coach on *The Afternoon Show*, is one of the top NLP Master Trainers around.

Owen and Brian are highly recommended by Dr Richard Bandler (co-founder of NLP) and the Society of NLP, the largest and oldest NLP Training Body in the world. They are known for their remarkable ability to work seamlessly together, and with great humour. Their unique training style reveals their great friendship and complementary methods.

Since they founded the institute they have taught NLP trainings in Ireland and Scotland. They provide regular NLP Evenings, Life-Enhancement Weekends, Art of Charisma Workshops, Trance Tripping, NLP Practitioners, NLP Business Practitioners, NLP Master Practitioners and NLP Coaching Programmes.

Owen and Brian also do corporate consulting and present in-house training to the corporate sector in the areas of communication, sales, motivation, stress management, creativity and business applications of NLP. To learn NLP in Ireland or to make your life and business better, visit the website today.

Irish Institute of NLP
84 Sundrive Road,
Kimmage, Dublin 12,
Ireland.

Tel: +353 (1) 490 2923
website: www.nlp.ie   email: info@nlp.ie

GENERAL INDEX

INDEX OF TIPS

INDEX OF EXERCISES / TECHNIQUES

Free postage[*]
Worldwide
on our web site
www.poolbeg.com

Direct to your home!

If you enjoyed this book why
not visit our website

and get another book delivered straight
to your home or to a friend's home!

www.poolbeg.com

All orders are despatched within 24 hours

* See web site for details